Written *on Our* Hearts

For Sarah
May His word find a place
in your heart!
Emily Freeman

Also by Emily Freeman

21 Days Closer to Christ

Keepers of What Matters Most

A Christ-Centered Christmas

Love Life, and See Good Days

Becoming His

Written on Our Hearts

Invitations from the Old Testament

Emily Freeman

Illustrations by Dan Burr

Deseret Book
Salt Lake City, Utah

In January 2012 a group of people
set off on a life-changing journey.
This book is dedicated to each of those travelers.

Visit us at DeseretBook.com

Library of Congress Cataloging-in-Publication Data
Freeman, Emily, author.
Written on our hearts : invitations from the Old Testament / Emily Freeman.
pages cm
Includes bibliographical references and index.
ISBN 978-1-60907-595-8 (hardbound : alk. paper)
1. Bible. Old Testament—Devotional literature. 2. The Church of Jesus Christ of Latter-day Saints—Doctrines. I. Title.
BS1151.55.F74 2013
221.6—dc23 2013019708

Printed in the United States of America
Publishers Printing, Salt Lake City, UT

10 9 8 7 6 5 4 3 2 1

contents

Acknowledgments

I once received a thank-you card that contained one handwritten line: *words cannot express . . .*

That is my sentiment as I begin to write this. Sometimes capturing words on paper is like wrestling; other times it is a process of discovery; and once in a while the words come as an unexpected gift. This book falls into the last category. The journey of coming to know the Deliverer is one of the most precious gifts I have ever received.

Heartfelt thanks to Jana Erickson for spending so much time helping me determine what was essential to include. Humble appreciation to my dear friend Emily Watts, who is a master at crafting the written word: Thank you for sharing your gift. I am profoundly grateful to the team at Deseret Book, including Heather Ward, Rachael Ward, and Sheryl Dickert Smith, for your attention to detail and the magical way you have of transforming words on a page into an experience for the heart. To Annie Henrie, whose cover artwork expresses so beautifully the spirit of this book. To Dan Burr, whose skill for capturing pure emotion on a simple piece of paper is a talent I greatly admire. To David Butler, whose wisdom, insight, and understanding led me to discover knowledge I couldn't have found on my own. To my mom and dad, and to the friends at www.dailyclosertochrist.com for accompanying me on this journey. To Meg and Grace, who gathered at 9:30 every night to share their favorite part. To Caleb, Josh, and Garett, who taught me the true meaning of sacrifice. And to Greg, who is my everything and my all in all. Without each of you this adventure would not have been complete.

Words cannot express . . .

introduction

People often ask me why I love the Old Testament so fiercely. I always respond with the same answer. There will come a moment in your life when you or someone you love will struggle with a challenge so great you will wonder how you will make it through. In that moment you will long to better understand the Savior's role as the Deliverer, and to do that you must go to the book of scripture that describes that role the best—the Old Testament. The stories and lessons of the Old Testament have carried me through some of the greatest challenges of my life. In those moments, much-needed verses of scripture have been written on my heart. When I need deeper courage, unyielding strength, and increased wisdom to face the situation at hand, I turn to the pages of the Old Testament. It is within those pages that I have come to know Jehovah, the Deliverer—Jesus Christ—in a way I might not have before.

Sometimes we glance through the chapters of the Old Testament and immediately feel intimidated by the sheer number of pages, the scriptural language, or even some of the harsh themes. I hope that won't be the case as we begin this study of the Old Testament. Instead, let anticipation begin to fill your heart—you are about to discover stories you might have missed and heroes you have never met before. This book is different from other Old Testament books you might have studied. It is not a verse-by-verse guide, nor will we delve deeply into the doctrine. Instead we will read the stories, looking for the inspiration within. As we do this, something remarkable will begin to happen—we will come to understand the great application these biblical stories can have in our lives today. The pages of the Old Testament include lessons on building testimony, strengthening family, following the prophet, overcoming great adversity, instilling belief, understanding hope, and finding the courage to sustain us through the great battles of life. We will learn how to trust with Gideon, build with Nehemiah, plead with Hezekiah, and stand up for what we know like Micaiah. We will read stories of courageous prophetesses, great women, and mothers in Israel. We will come to understand the importance of the scarlet thread, the fringes, and what it means to be wise hearted. We will realize that the greatest blessings in life cannot come from that which doth cost us nothing.

We live in a world that pleads for deliverance. We may not be called upon to cross the Red Sea, find ourselves thrown into a pit and left for dead, or face armies whose strength is far greater than ours. We may not be led into captivity, be compassed on every side by the enemy, or be called upon to testify knowing it might lead to our death. However, there will be days when we face danger, oppression, and injustice. There will be great obstacles in our way and times when we feel surrounded by those who are intent on destroying us. We will face evil, overwhelming health challenges, and perhaps the captivity of sin. In these moments we must remember that, just as the Lord delivered the children of Israel, He has the power to deliver us from any trouble we must overcome in our life. He is, after all, the Great Deliverer. The pages of the Old Testament testify of Him.

In the midst of every challenge or adversity, one thing is certain—the Lord *will* deliver us. The Old Testament will help us understand how.

And these words . . . shall be in thine heart:
and thou shalt teach them diligently
unto thy children,
and shalt talk of them
when thou sittest in thine house,
and when thou walkest by the way,
and when thou liest down,
and when thou risest up.

DEUTERONOMY 6:6–7

"Because thou hast done this thing,
and hast not withheld thy son, thine only son:
That in blessing I will bless thee . . ."

GENESIS 22:16–17

Invitations from

The First Book of Moses Called Genesis

A Reminder

Is it true, I wonder, that every time God created something, He stood back and knew that it was good? We read it in the second chapter of Moses: "And I, God, saw that all things which I had created were good" (Moses 2:21). Then again, in the third chapter of Abraham just before the Creation: "He stood among those that were spirits, and he saw that they were good" (Abraham 3:23). Once more in the first chapter of Genesis: "And God saw every thing that he had made, and, behold, it was very good" (Genesis 1:31).

I believe that when the scriptures teach us something with repetition, it must be a principle the Lord wants us to remember and never forget. What is it about that doctrine that is so important it needed to be repeated three times? Consider this—God created you. Which means He knows that you are good. And not just good, *very good.* He believes that about you, even on your worst days.

So when things don't seem to be going exactly right, when the whole world seems to be crashing down around you, when you aren't quite sure if you are any good at anything, you might want to turn to Moses, or Abraham, or Genesis, and be reminded, *God saw every thing that he had made, and, behold, it was very good.* Every thing.

On the days you are in particular need of that reminder, maybe you could also gain strength from one more lesson that is repeated in all three chapters. "And I, God, created man in mine own image . . . male and female created I them. And I, God, *blessed them*" (Moses 2:27–28; emphasis added). "So the Gods went down to organize man in their own image . . . male and female to form they them. And the Gods said: *We will bless them*" (Abraham 4:27–28; emphasis added). "So God created man in his own image, in the image of God created he him; male and female created he them. *And God blessed them*" (Genesis 1:27–28; emphasis added).

What is the good God sees in you? Can you think of one simple gift He has blessed you with for which you are most grateful?

The profound thought of God creating us, knowing the good in each of us, and then blessing us gives me courage, and strength, and hope. Never forget: You are good. You are blessed. It is right there in the scriptures, almost like a letter from home.

A reminder of God's love.

comfort ye your Hearts

There is a lesson to be learned in the plains of Mamre from the moment when three holy men appeared to Abraham. In that moment, Abraham realized these holy men had the power to bless his life. He was not going to let that opportunity pass him by. As the men approached Abraham, he said, "Pass not away. . . . Let a little water, I pray you, be fetched, and wash your feet, and rest yourselves under the tree: And I will fetch a morsel of bread, and *comfort ye your hearts*. . . . And they said, So do, as thou hast said" (Genesis 18:3–5; emphasis added).

I couldn't help but notice the way in which Abraham performed their request: "And Abraham *hastened* into the tent unto Sarah, and said, Make ready *quickly* three measures of fine meal. . . . And Abraham *ran* unto the herd, and fetcht a calf . . . and he *hasted* to dress it . . . and *he stood by them* under the tree, and they did eat" (Genesis 18:6–8; emphasis added).

There are holy men in my life—bishops, stake presidents, Apostles, and a prophet of the Lord. I have pondered the way in which I go and do what the holy men in my life have asked of me. Do I *hasten* to perform their counsel? Do I *quickly* respond? In a world that mocks and questions and throws stones, do I *stand by them?*

Abraham and Sarah's choice to follow these holy men led to a miraculous blessing in their life—one that could not have been realized without intervention from the Lord. I wonder, What miraculous blessing does the Lord hold in store for me? In the moments when I wonder *how* and *if* those blessings will ever come to fruition, I will take counsel from these words found in Genesis 18:19, "For I know him, that he will command his children and his household after him, and they shall keep the way of the Lord . . . *that the Lord may bring upon Abraham that which he hath spoken of him.*" From Abraham we learn that choosing to keep the way of the Lord enables Him to bring upon us that which He has spoken, to fulfill His great promise, to shower blessings upon us.

Consider the counsel given in the last general conference. What quote comforted your heart most?

I love the reassurance the Lord gave to Abraham, "Is any thing *too hard* for the Lord?" (Genesis 18:14; emphasis added). We must follow the footnote next to *hard* for the answer. The verses we are led to speak of Abraham, "Who against hope believed in hope, . . . and being not weak in faith, . . . he staggered not at the promise of God . . . but was strong in faith . . . being *fully persuaded* that, what [God] had promised, he was able also to perform" (Romans 4:18–21; emphasis added).

From Abraham's story I learn that choosing to follow the counsel from holy men has the power to bless my life. In the moments when my heart needs comfort, in the moments when I am lost and wandering, in the moments when I question if the Lord has any great blessing in store for me, I will *haste* to follow their words *quickly,* knowing I will be led closer to the Lord. He will bring comfort and healing, He will offer direction and counsel, He will send peace and strength, and He will bring the miracles—that which He has spoken. Nothing is too hard for the Lord.

The Road to Moriah

As I consider the journey that took place on the road to Moriah, I ponder the thoughts that must have filled Abraham's heavy heart. "Take now thy son, thine only son Isaac, whom thou lovest" (Genesis 22:2). I imagine the sun rising early that morning, the gathering of the wood, the planning for the three-day journey ahead. I think of the thoughts that must have filled Abraham's heart every time he lifted his eyes to see the place afar off. I imagine the last stretch of that journey, as Abraham climbed the mountain with his son—his only son, whom he loved. When he came to the place God had told him of, I picture him building the altar somberly with his own hands and carefully laying out the wood, each piece in order. It is beyond my capacity to understand what he must have felt as he gently bound his trusting, obedient son and laid him on the altar.

And then, when Abraham stretched forth his hand, an angel called unto him—in the very moment when it became clear that Abraham would not withhold anything from the Lord. When asked why God commanded Abraham to sacrifice Isaac, President Hugh B. Brown suggested it was because "Abraham needed to learn something about Abraham" (in Truman G. Madsen, *The Highest in Us*, 49). I wonder, What is it I need to learn about myself? What am I willing to give to the Lord to learn that lesson? What am I willing to sacrifice?

After reading about Abraham, I realize that I must become more willing to take the journey, to climb the mountain, to withhold nothing—even when I don't know what the end of the path will bring. "Each time I walk with Abraham and Isaac on the road to Mount Moriah, I weep, knowing that Abraham does not know that there will be an angel and a ram in the thicket at the end of the journey. We are each in the middle of our earthly path, and we don't know the end of our own stories. But we, as Abraham, are blessed with miracles" (Susan W. Tanner, "My Soul Delighteth," 82–83).

The road to Moriah is a road filled with sacrifice. But it is also a road filled with miracles. A favorite hymn reminds me, "Sacrifice brings forth the blessings of heaven" ("Praise to the Man," *Hymns,* no. 27). I think of Abraham, and my heart knows the truth of that phrase.

As Abraham and Isaac prepared to leave Mount Moriah, the angel called unto Abraham a second time, saying, "Because thou hast done this thing, and hast not withheld thy son, thine only son: that in blessing I will bless thee . . . because thou hast obeyed my voice" (Genesis 22:16–18).

What does your sacrifice look like?

What are the stones you lift every day?

What is the bundle of wood you carry?

I will never forget preparing to send our second son on a mission. His service has been one of the neatest experiences in our lives, but it has also been one of the greatest sacrifices. Josh was diagnosed with diabetes when he was three years old. I have worried about his mission every day since he was diagnosed. The health implications made me so nervous. But we prepared for that day, and by the time Josh sent in his papers, his doctors felt he was ready to go.

The night before he left for the Missionary Training Center, we finished packing his suitcases, laid out his suit for the next day, and went to bed. At 4:00 a.m. I heard some noise in the kitchen. I walked in to find him eating a bowl of cereal and making a peanut-butter-and-jam sandwich. "What are you doing?" I asked.

"My blood sugar is 43," he replied. I sat in the kitchen and talked to him as he ate, making sure that his numbers went back to where they needed to be. Then he went to bed and I went to my room and cried. Who would take care of him for the next two years? When his numbers were low, who would sit up in the kitchen and make sure he had enough to eat? I prayed that the Lord would bless him with companions who would be mindful.

I wonder, What is it I need to learn about myself? What am I willing to give to the Lord to learn that lesson? What am I willing to sacrifice?

The next morning I took my son, my second son Josh, whom I love, and dropped him off on the curb at the MTC. In that moment, in a very small way, I knew what it meant to withhold nothing from the Lord.

In the Mount Moriah moments of our lives, in the moments when we choose to withhold nothing from the Lord, in the moments of greatest sacrifice, perhaps we could try to remember that in His own way and in His own time, the Lord will provide the angel and the ram in the thicket. When all is said and done, He will withhold nothing from us. In blessing He will bless us. May our eyes be open to recognize those blessings.

Happily Ever After

You should pop some popcorn before you read this. Settle in. Put your feet up. Then prepare your heart; you are about to read one of the best love scenes in the scriptures.

In Genesis 24 we are introduced to Rebekah, a damsel with a kind heart. How do we know her heart was kind? "And the servant ran to meet her, and said, Let me, I pray thee, drink a little water of thy pitcher. And she said, Drink, my lord: and she hasted, and let down her pitcher upon her hand, and gave him drink. And when she had done giving him drink, she said, *I will draw water for thy camels also, until they have done drinking*" (Genesis 24:17–19; emphasis added). Do you know how much a camel can drink? Up to twenty gallons in one sitting! Out of the goodness of her heart, Rebekah offered to draw water for the servant's camels with her pitcher—*until they were done drinking.* That's what kind of heart Rebekah had.

Rebekah, with a kind heart, is about to be introduced to Isaac, who was loved much, who was obedient, and who was trustworthy. (This is the part when you need the soundtrack—preferably one with violins and a cello.) "Isaac went out to meditate in the field at the eventide: and he lifted up his eyes, and saw, and, behold, the camels were coming. And Rebekah lifted up her eyes, and when she saw Isaac, she lighted off the camel. For she had said unto the servant, What man is this that walketh in the field to meet us?" (Genesis 24:63–65). Sadly, the scripture account leaves out the introduction, the courtship, and the details of the wedding—but we do know this: "She became his wife; *and he loved her*" (Genesis 24:67; emphasis added). He loved her. Three simple words that evoke powerful emotion—*he loved her.* It makes my heart so happy to know that Isaac loved Rebekah, the damsel with the kind heart. I smiled the entire time I read those verses, and they made me so happy the first time, I actually went back and read them again.

> She became his wife, and he loved her. Why is having a kind heart essential to a marriage?

It's a love story, a fairy tale filled with adventure, romance, courage, hope, and everlasting love, right there in the book of Genesis.

As President Dieter F. Uchtdorf said of fairy tales: "I love it when we turn to the last page and our eyes reach the final lines and we see the enchanting words 'And they lived happily ever after.' . . . The day will come when you turn the final pages of your own glorious story; there you will read and experience the fulfillment of those blessed and wonderful words" ("Your Happily Ever After," 124, 127).

I believe that with all my heart.

I really do.

second chances

Recently I went to one of my daughter's basketball games. In a very intense moment of the game, just after a turnover, Meg's coach called for a time out. He waited until he had the complete focus of the five players who had come off the floor, and then he said, "I'm not worried about you making mistakes. I know you are going to make mistakes. It's what you do after the mistake that I care about. It's how you recover."

I watched that interaction from the stands and knew I had just been taught a lesson that was profound. What was true in a basketball game was also true in life. What we do after we make mistakes—the way in which we recover from those mistakes—can often become the defining element of our lives.

I printed up that quote from my daughter's coach and hung it in my basement. I want my children to know this is what I believe. They will probably make a mistake or two—in fact, I know they will. But I also know that a loving Father in Heaven prepared a way for them to recover from those mistakes by providing a Savior. I believe in the power of the Atonement. I believe in second chances.

The story of Jacob in the book of Genesis is filled with mistakes—life-altering mistakes: deceiving, adultery, stealing, and murder. Within the verses I see the wickedness of our time, and amidst the wickedness my heart longs for someone to choose good. Through the story of Jacob's life I learn a powerful lesson about making mistakes and recovering from them.

Alfred Edersheim, a Bible scholar, explains that Jacob's biggest mistake was that he tried to go before God. Rather than letting God orchestrate the events of his life, he tried to solve them with his own strength. Dangers and difficulties arose every time Jacob made that decision in his life. If we read carefully, we come to understand that God's dealings with Jacob show how mercifully, how wisely He removed this characteristic that had become a hindrance, how He uprooted those sins from Jacob's heart and his life. In Edersheim's words: "Such hours come to most of us, when it almost seems as if necessity obliged and holy wisdom prompted us to accomplish, *in our own strength,* that which, nevertheless, we should leave in God's hand. . . . Here faith is the only true remedy: faith, which leaves God to carry out His own purposes, content to trust Him absolutely, and to follow Him whithersoever He leadeth. And God's way is never through the thicket of human cunning and devices" (*Bible History,* 1:117; emphasis added).

One of the most powerful lessons we learn from Jacob is that every choice will eventually bring a consequence. It is not a coincidence that Jacob, who as a youth dressed up in goat skin to fool his father, was deceived by his father-in-law, who dressed up the wrong woman on his wedding night. The next morning when Jacob (who once deceived) woke up, he learned a powerful lesson on how it feels to be deceived.

From Jacob's story we begin to realize that the paths we walk in this life are not unknown or without design. Even the detours can be navigated to direct our path back toward the destination the Lord has in mind for us. I have great admiration for Jacob because he walked the same test of life that we all do and found the strength within to rise above his errors.

In my scriptures I have marked the moments when Jacob relied on his own strength, understanding, and devices, rather than upon the Lord's. I have tried to learn from his journey. I want to be more willing to let the Lord lead, to be patient, rather than to control my destiny by my own strength, to wrestle with the Lord through prayer, and in so doing to recognize that I *have* been blessed, that I do have enough (see Genesis 33:11). Most important, I have learned that the Lord knows that I, like Jacob, will make mistakes. What He watches for is what I do after a mistake . . . how I recover. In such times, will I be willing to use the Atonement? Am I willing to let Him change me for good?

I am learning that the Old Testament does not shy away from showing us the painful mistakes of others. It does not shield us from the stories of those whose choices destroyed their lives. My heart has broken over the choices of Dinah, Tamar, Lot's daughters, Simeon, and Levi, to name a few. But the Old Testament also teaches us that our God believes in second chances, and even third chances. He gives us every chance. He believes in moving past the mistake. He believes in helping us to become who He knows we can become.

> Do you believe in a god of second chances? How does that belief instill comfort?

In a day where we are surrounded by the devastating consequences of mistakes and sins such as the ones we read about in the Old Testament, I am grateful for this scriptural record that shows us the consequences of a choice—whether for good or for evil. I am grateful for the stories of men such as Jacob that teach us to learn from our mistakes, to believe in second chances, and to rely wholly upon the Lord.

Empty Your Sack

Have you ever noticed what happened each time the brothers left Joseph's home in Egypt during the famine?

The first time they left they stopped at an inn. "And it came to pass as they emptied their sacks, that, behold, every man's bundle of money was in his sack" (Genesis 42:35). Immediately they returned to Joseph and explained, "When we came to the inn, that *we opened our sacks,* and, behold, every man's money was in the mouth of his sack, *our money in full weight:* and we have brought it again in our hand. . . . We cannot tell who put our money in our sacks." And Joseph replied, "Peace be to you, fear not: your God, and the God of your father, hath given you treasure in your sacks" (Genesis 43:21–23; emphasis added).

As they prepared to leave for home the second time, Joseph "commanded the steward of his house, saying, Fill the men's sacks with food, *as much as they can carry,* and put every man's money in his sack's mouth" (Genesis 44:1; emphasis added). This time Joseph requested their sacks to be filled with not just enough to supply their needs, but more—much more.

The third time the brothers left, a sack was not sufficient for the treasure their brother had in store. Joseph sent wagons and ten horses laden with good things, along with ten more horses laden with corn, bread, and meat.

If Joseph is a type of Christ, then we have just been taught a very important characteristic of the Lord. We learn a little more about the Giver of Every Good Gift—who gives not just enough to simply supply our needs, but more. Much more.

My mind is focused on the image of ten brothers with sacks on their backs, ten brothers who, as they emptied their sacks, discovered treasure beyond their expectations. As I thought about this principle, I wondered what I might discover if I were to figuratively empty my sack to discover the treasure the Lord has given me. So I tried it. The contents surpassed my expectations.

> If you were to take a moment to empty your sack today, what would you discover?

As I emptied my sack, I took counsel from the advice Pharaoh gave the brothers as they returned home to bring their father back to Egypt: "*Regard not your stuff;* for the good of all the land of Egypt is yours" (Genesis 45:20, emphasis added). So I didn't count my *stuff.* Instead I tried to discover those things that would be considered good in the eyes of the Lord. This type of treasure requires thought to discern. I pondered on the gifts of time, freedom, the fruits of hard labor, truths restored, the power of the priesthood in my life, covenants I have made, people I love, prayers answered, and tender mercies.

I was surprised to discover that the sweetest treasures were those that required the most sacrifice. Interestingly, the emptier my sack became, the fuller became my heart. Within the emptying I came to understand that I have been truly blessed. It's been a long time since I have taken a good look at the treasure I have been given from the Lord. Through this exercise I realized the Lord has truly given me as much as I can carry, and I find myself echoing the words of Jacob: "It is enough" (Genesis 45:28).

Am I in the Place of God?

I remember well the day my prayers were focused on the boy down the street who was having heart surgery. I prayed constantly, and as I prayed I pondered. I could have wondered why: Why the broken heart? Why the surgery after surgery after surgery? Why the mother's faith tested and proved sufficient—again? But instead my heart learned from Joseph and the power of the lesson found at the very end of Genesis.

In the moment when Joseph's brothers came pleading, asking forgiveness for the great trial they had imposed upon him, he could have turned to them and said, "Why the pit, why the bag of silver in place of a brother, why the years in prison?" Instead he asked them a profound question, "Am I in the place of God?" (Genesis 50:19).

It was as if he was saying, "In the end, isn't the place where I ended up after all those trials the exact place God needed me to be?" Think about it. Had there not been the pit, the slavery, the years in prison, there would not have been the opportunity for leadership, for saving a nation, for saving his family. The truth of it is, the trial was what enabled him to be in the place God needed him to be.

I love this line: "As for you, ye thought evil against me; but God meant it unto good, to bring to pass, as it is this day, to save much people alive" (Genesis 50:20). What a profound message. Joseph experienced a trial that had the potential to destroy him, but God meant it unto good. God *turned it* unto good.

Think of the greatest trial in your life. Looking back, can you see how God meant it unto you for good? If you can't see it now, perhaps you might ask that He will open your heart to understand.

In the midst of our greatest trials, we need to make sure we are asking the right question. Asking *why* might not help us discover the answer we are truly seeking. Maybe the right question to ask in the midst of tribulation is the one Joseph asked: "Am I in the place of God?" We may not understand the trials we face in this life, particularly when we are in the midst of them. But we can always trust that God can turn them to our good.

> Have you been in the place of God? Looking back, can you see how God meant it for your good?

Just before lunch I received a text from the boy's mother. The surgery went well. The boy was resting comfortably in the ICU. The next line in the text said, "Let Rejoicing Go Unrestrained!" I knew immediately she was in the place of God. As hard as this journey has been, and as hard as it surely will be, she knows God means it for her good and for her son's good. In the midst of greatest trial, she has found moments to rejoice unrestrained.

"Put off thy shoes from off thy feet,
for the place whereon thou standest is holy ground."

Exodus 3:5

Invitations from

The Second Book of Moses Called Exodus, The Third Book of Moses Called Leviticus, and The Fourth Book of Moses Called Numbers

Bring Your Finest

Near my house, there is a huge field that sits vacant all through the year. No one plants on it and no one waters it. Most of the time it is covered in dry weeds and baked mud. But not every day. One day when I drove by I found it covered with beautiful yellow flowers. I thought to myself, *Can beauty be found in wilderness places?*

When I read chapter 25 of Exodus, my thoughts fill with beauty as the descriptions of the finery brought to build the tabernacle are listed. This chapter talks of blue, purple, and scarlet fabric, along with fine linen. It mentions rings of pure gold and adornments of silver and brass and precious stones. "Speak unto the children of Israel, that they bring me an offering: of every man that giveth it willingly with his heart ye shall take my offering. . . . And let them make me a sanctuary; that I may dwell among them" (Exodus 25:2, 8).

I am reminded that the Israelites are in the wilderness, and I ask myself again, *Can beauty be found in wilderness places?* I realize the offering will require sacrifice—giving up, and giving all. The people cannot purchase what will be required for the sanctuary in the wilderness. Building the tabernacle will require them to bring their own finery to the Lord.

Through this bringing of their finest there is a process of sanctification taking place, and a process of consecration. I study *sanctification* in the dictionary: To make religious. To free from sin. To set apart.

I see that it comes from Latin *sanctus,* which means "holy." I realize that sanctification includes giving up in the sense of letting go. Next I study *consecration:* To make sacred. To devote something exclusively to a particular purpose. To dedicate. I see that it comes from Latin *consecrat,* which means "dedicated" or "devoted," and from Latin *sacer,* which means "sacred." "Dedicated sacred." I come to understand that consecration includes giving all in the sense of giving everything.

This bringing of their finest would require Israel to become dedicated. Devoted. The sacrifice would build a sanctuary that was sacred to them—one that would make them holy through the process of letting go and giving everything.

What is one way that you could bring your finest to the Lord?

As I consider this path toward sanctification, toward consecration, toward holiness, I want to understand what it means to bring my finest as an offering to the Lord. Israel has been asked to walk in obedience in preparation for the covenant they are about to make with the Lord. It is hard work, this walking in obedience. But the Father knows walking in obedience includes making mistakes, and He has provided One to plead in our behalf. It is through the process of obedience, of repentance, of sacrificing, giving up, and letting go, that we become sanctified. Then, as we bring our finest offering and give it *willingly* with our heart, through giving all, we become consecrated.

Through the process we are dedicated sacred and we are made holy—in preparation. For when Israel arrives at that place of sanctification, that place of consecration, the Lord has given a promise: "And there I will meet with thee, and I will commune with thee" (Exodus 25:22).

one step backward

When you read about the wickedness that took place while Moses was on Mount Sinai, do you find yourself asking how could this have happened?

Why was Israel so quick to forget the bondage, the plagues, the parting of the Red Sea? The cloud by day and the pillar of light in the wilderness? How about the manna, which surely would have kept appearing every morning of the forty mornings Moses was upon the mount. Did they become too commonplace, these miracles in the midst of the ordinary? Is it so hard to walk forward, to follow the Lord, to obey?

"Go, get thee down; for thy people, which thou broughtest out of the land of Egypt, have corrupted themselves: They have turned aside quickly out of the way which I commanded them" (Exodus 32:7–8). I can't help but focus on one phrase: *They have turned aside quickly out of the way.* I am discouraged by Israel's choice. Really discouraged. Then I take a good, hard look at my own life and I realize, *I do that.* Sometimes I turn aside quickly out of the way because moving from where I am to where I need to be is often harder than I thought. I make the choice for the better. I feel the confirmation as I press forward. But then the stretching becomes painful. Staying the course becomes exhausting. I look at where I was before and it seems familiar, easier, and more comfortable. So I turn aside. Just for a little break. It can happen so quickly.

For just one moment I can understand Israel's fear that their prophet had disappeared and wasn't going to come back. I can understand the disappointment in the eyes of a brother as he asks, "What did this people unto thee, that thou hast brought so great a sin upon them?" (Exodus 32:21). I can hear Moses begging the Lord to give Israel another try, a second chance. I know that fear, that disappointment, that discouragement, that plea. I love how the Lord answers Moses, "I will do this thing also that thou hast spoken: for thou hast found grace in my sight, and I know thee by name" (Exodus 33:17).

Have there been moments in your life when you have turned aside quickly? In those moments, what gave you the strength to move forward rather than taking one step backward?

My thoughts fill with grace, and I realize how it applies to sanctification. The Bible Dictionary explains that grace is a divine means of help or strength, an enabling power after we have expended our own best efforts, assistance that we otherwise would not be able to maintain if left to our own means (see Bible Dictionary, s.v. "Grace"). Immediately one thing becomes clear to me: I do not have to move from where I am to where I need to be alone or by my own means. The Lord will press forward with me. When the stretching becomes painful, He will be my help and my strength. When staying the course exhausts me, He will become my enabling power. He knows me. He knows my name. I am not alone. There is comfort in that knowledge. Therein I find strength. So this time I will move forward with the Lord by my side, "having not the smallest desire to go one step backward" (Mary Fielding Smith, in Corbett, *Mary Fielding Smith,* 100).

A clear path

Sometimes the path is clearly marked. Black and white. On the asphalt near my children's elementary school is a painted crosswalk, denoting a place of safety. The same is true in the book of Leviticus, in chapter 18, where the Lord cautions against nakedness. The first time I read through this chapter I wondered how it applied to our day. It just wasn't clear at first. But after I spent some time pondering, the realization dawned.

The caution that makes up chapter 18 is the stuff that makes up our day. It fills the sitcoms and movies and novels. We see it on the news. We find it on the Internet. It is there, all around us. With the touch of a button, everything the Lord has cautioned against in the eighteenth chapter of Leviticus can permeate the walls of our own homes. I turn back to the chapter intent on learning what the Lord was trying to teach Israel.

At the start, I begin to see the path of safety. "I am the Lord your God. After the doings of the land of Egypt, wherein ye dwelt, shall ye not do: and after the doings of the land of Canaan, whither I bring you, shall ye not do: *neither shall ye walk* in their ordinances" (Leviticus 18:2–3; emphasis added). On the one hand, do not be Egypt. Let go of your past sins. Do not walk the path they trod. On the other hand, do not be Canaan. There will be days of temptation ahead of you. Do not follow their footsteps. It becomes clear, black and white—this path I should not walk.

What follows these verses is the counsel that will guide my steps: "Ye shall do my judgments, and keep mine ordinances, *to walk therein:* I am the Lord your God. . . . Keep my statutes . . . which if a man do, he shall live in them: I am the Lord" (Leviticus 18:4–5; emphasis added). My thoughts fill with judgments and statutes and ordinances.

The Lord has provided the path for us to walk in. But it is hard work, this walking the clear path. It's black and white—to walk out of the movie unfinished, to set down the novel unread, to turn off a favorite sitcom without rationalizing "that one part."

How will walking in the way of the Lord make you a peculiar treasure?

Sometimes I feel alone on this path. Separate. Peculiar. But I am reminded of the promise of the Lord, "If ye will obey my voice indeed, and keep my covenant, then ye shall be *a peculiar treasure* unto me . . . and ye shall be unto me . . . an holy nation" (Exodus 19:5–6; emphasis added). I cannot be Egypt. I cannot be Canaan. I must choose to be a holy nation. I must be Israel. A peculiar people. Separate. If I truly want to understand the way of the Lord, if I truly want to walk therein, I must follow His path of safety. It's black and white.

My whole soul

When I read the scriptures, I have several goals. I want to find something every day that will apply to my life, change me in some way, lift my heart, or strengthen my belief. But more than anything, I just want to come to know the Lord a little better than I know Him now. So every day as I read the verses I look for Him there.

I try to be humble as I search for the lesson within the reading—willing to change, to give my heart, to find strength in the words. One example is Leviticus 22:18–19, "Speak . . . unto all the children of Israel, and say unto them, Whatsoever he be of the house of Israel . . . that will offer his oblation . . . unto the Lord . . . ye shall offer at your own will." I wonder, *What is my offering to the Lord?* I do not have a lamb without a blemish, or a bullock that I might bring. I look back to the verses to try to discover the learning. What is here that applies to my life?

"In me is the law of Moses fulfilled. . . . Ye shall offer up unto me no more the shedding of blood; yea, your sacrifices and your burnt offerings shall be done away. . . . And ye shall offer for a sacrifice unto me a broken heart and a contrite spirit. . . . Behold, for such I have laid down my life." (3 Nephi 9:17, 19–20, 22).

My heart knows what it is to be broken. The aching. The tearstains. The time spent on my knees waiting for healing to come. My spirit knows what it is to be contrite. The regret. The wearing down. The longing to be made whole. Does He really want this broken heart? This spirit worn down? I search to understand more of this offering He asks for, and the footnotes lead me to the exhortation of Amaleki, "And now, my beloved brethren, I would that ye should come unto Christ, who is the Holy One of Israel . . . yea, come unto him, and *offer your whole souls* as an offering unto him" (Omni 1:26; emphasis added). I realize He wants more than just my heart to mend and my spirit to heal. He wants my *whole soul*—all of me. That offering is going to require trust and sacrifice. *My whole soul.* My heart. My might. My mind. My strength.

Consider the offering requested of us in this chapter of Leviticus:
Become holy,
Live righteously,
Love your neighbor,
Keep the commandments.
Knowing this, what could you offer the Lord?

I wonder if that is what Israel felt in this moment of the journey in Leviticus, if they understood what it meant to really give their heart, to give their soul. Had they experienced enough of the aching, the tearstains, the time spent on their knees, the spirit worn down, the regret? Were they finally humble enough to trust the Lord who had brought them out of Egypt? Because now the offering He asked of Israel was that they become holy, live righteously, love their neighbor, and keep the commandments. My heart recognizes these as offerings of the soul. The whole soul.

I find myself considering my offering to the Lord, to become holy, to live righteously, to love my neighbor, to keep the commandments. I must do this with all of my heart, my mind, my might, my strength. I want to offer my best. I want to give my "first fruits," my broken heart, my spirit worn down.

I want to give Him my whole soul.

The Fringes

One evening my family was invited to a celebration held on a high mountain overlooking the valley below, with friends who had come to remember. We spoke reverently of a sweet girl born on that February day two years before. She was privileged to spend a few hours with her tender mother, doting father, dear sister, and brave brothers. Just long enough to leave a gentle impression on their hearts, and then she returned home to heaven.

Today was her birthday. In honor of her memory, her mother asked that we write down a celebration in our life and tie it to the end of a balloon, because in this mother's heart her dear, sweet baby will always be remembered as a celebration.

Our thoughts were drawn inward as we pondered happy things. Then we wrote down our celebrations on pale pink cards and tied each one with a bright bow to the end of a pink balloon. We stood there in a circle and sang softly, a gentle melody with words to remind us that families can be forever. The testimony of that truth burned through my heart and streamed in wet tears down my cheeks. Then the baby's mother asked us to let go of our balloons, in celebration, and as we remembered our eyes lifted heavenward.

In the book of Numbers, Moses teaches a lesson on the importance of remembering. "Speak unto the children of Israel, and bid them that they make them fringes in the borders of their garments . . . that they put upon the fringe of the borders a ribband of blue: And it shall be unto you for a fringe, that ye may look upon it, and remember all the commandments of the Lord, and do them; and that ye seek not after your own heart . . . that ye may remember, and do all my commandments, and be holy" (Numbers 15:38–40). I love this thought of fringes. Do we have fringes today? Are there tangible things, like the pink balloons, that can lead our hearts to remember and our eyes to draw heavenward?

What are some of the fringes in your home? Would you like to add more?

I wanted to think that I might have such things, so after reading that verse I wandered around my house looking for fringes—reminders placed around my home that would help me remember all the commandments of the Lord. Up the stairway, I saw the reminder of our family mission statement. In the family room there were three brass keys representing family prayer, family home evening, and family scripture study. There was a picture of the temple in my daughter's room, a favorite painting of the Savior in the front hall, a Personal Progress necklace lying on the dresser, and general conference quotes hanging on the wall. As I wandered, I began to realize that we have placed fringes all around us—simple reminders quietly prompting us to consider the commandments, to lift our hearts heavenward.

"And it shall be unto you for a fringe, that ye may look upon it, and remember" (Numbers 15:39).

"What mean ye by these stones?"

Joshua 4:6

Invitations from

The Fifth Book of Moses Called Deuteronomy, The Book of Joshua, The Book of Judges, and The Book of Ruth

chosen

Being married to a lacrosse coach has taught me that tryouts are just as stressful for a coach as they are for the players. The coach loses sleep over this. He spends a lot of time thinking about each boy. Making the team requires more than just talent. Dedication and commitment are considered. The coach doesn't just choose the boys with the *most* talent. Sometimes he chooses the ones with the *least talent but the most dedication.*

This coaching, it's not about the winning for him. He will tell you it is, but I will tell you it's not. It's about the boys. He teaches them respect, honor on the field and off, and how to become champions in the game so they can become champions in life. He spends a lot of time on this. The boys learn to honor him by honoring the game. It doesn't take long to realize that he loves every one of those boys.

One night he posted two lists: a varsity squad, and a JV squad. It was hard making the separation. I watched him fret over it for hours. But the thing I love about the coach and his team tryout is this: Everyone who tried out for the team made it onto one list or the other. No one was cut. He chose to keep every single boy because he believes in the potential of each player.

It reminds me of some of the verses in Deuteronomy: "For thou art an holy people unto the Lord thy God: the Lord thy God hath chosen thee to be a special people unto himself, above all people that are upon the face of the earth. The Lord did not set his love upon you, nor choose you, *because ye were more* in number than any people; *for ye were the fewest* of all people: But because the Lord loved you . . . hath [he] brought you out with a mighty hand" (Deuteronomy 7:6–8; emphasis added). "And he will love thee, and bless thee, and multiply thee. . . . Thou shalt be blessed above all people" (Deuteronomy 7:13–14). The Lord didn't choose Israel because they were more, because in reality they were the fewest. He did what He did for them because He loved them. That's why He was faithful to them. He believed in their potential—enough to bring them out of captivity with a mighty hand. I believe He will do the same for us.

> How does it make you feel to know that the Lord has chosen you for who you are? What does He see in you?

Do you ever have one of those days when you look back and wonder if you are enough? If you gave your best? If anyone recognized your effort? Do you wonder whose team you are on? If anyone is cheering for you? On those days, maybe you could remember these verses. The Lord has chosen you because He thinks you are special. You don't have to be more than anyone else; you can be numbered among the fewest. He will still choose you. He loves you. He won't turn you away. The Lord thy God, He is God, the faithful God, who has promised that you will be blessed among all people. Believe Him. There is nothing that would make Him happier than to know that you are on His team.

He knows your potential.

He has chosen you.

Choose Him.

Let It Suffice Thee

I have become attached to Moses. This journey through the wilderness has given me a great love and respect for a man I knew very little about before we started. I must admit, saying farewell to him tugs at my heartstrings.

The last part of Numbers and Deuteronomy is hard to take in. Do you find it hard to fathom why Moses wasn't the prophet who led Israel on the last stretch of the journey over Jordan and into the promised land? Our hearts wonder if it is fair. We might argue that he *earned* the right. Perhaps we question the decision conveyed to Moses from the Lord. But from this moment we learn an important lesson—God's will for His children is good. Always. We must trust that principle even when we don't understand it.

"And the Lord said unto Moses, Get thee up into this mount . . . and *see the land* which I have given unto the children of Israel. And when thou hast seen it, thou also shalt be gathered unto thy people" (Numbers 27:12–13; emphasis added). It is touching to see how meekly Moses received this direction from the Lord. When he realized he wouldn't lead the people into the promised land, his chief concern was that God would appoint a suitable successor for His people. The Lord honored that request and instructed him to appoint Joshua to lead Israel.

Scripture records, with touching simplicity, what passed then between Moses and the Lord. "O Lord God, *thou hast begun* to shew thy servant thy greatness, and thy mighty hand: for what God is there in heaven or in earth, that can do according to thy works, and according to thy might? I pray thee, let me go over, and see the good land that is beyond Jordan . . . and the Lord said unto me, *Let it suffice thee;* speak no more unto me of this matter" (Deuteronomy 3:24–26; emphasis added).

Two phrases within that verse stand out to me: *thou hast begun* and *let it suffice thee.*

First, we learn that in 120 years Moses had *just begun* to see the greatness of the Lord—which leads me to understand that he must have known the Lord still had great things in store for him. Second, I love the words *let it suffice thee.* It is as if the Lord was saying, *This is enough. Find joy in this much and then trust me.* The scriptures record that even though Moses would not lead the people into the promised land, he did have the privilege of seeing it. "Then, amid the respectful silence of a mourning people, [Moses] set out alone upon his last pilgrim-journey. All the way up to the highest top of Pisgah the eyes of the people must have followed him. They could watch him as he stood there in the sunset, taking his full view of the land—there to see for himself how true and faithful Jehovah had been" (Alfred Edersheim, *Bible History,* 3:43).

> "Let it suffice thee . . ."
> Can you think of a moment in your life when those four words would have brought you comfort?

When we think of Moses, we must remember that God prepared something better for him than even entrance into the land of earthly promise. From his story we learn that sometimes the Lord prepares a different ending from what we had envisioned, but it is always the right ending.

Become a possibilitarian

"When thou goest out . . . be not afraid . . . for the Lord thy God is with thee. . . . Let not your hearts faint, fear not, and do not tremble, neither be ye terrified. . . . For the Lord your God is he that goeth with you" (Deuteronomy 20:1, 3–4).

If you don't mind, I would like to introduce you to a possibilitarian. What is a possibilitarian, you ask? I love the definition often attributed to Norman Vincent Peale: "Become a possibilitarian. No matter how dark things seem to be or actually are, raise your sights and see possibilities—always see them, for they're always there." One of the greatest possibilitarians of all time was Joshua, the prophet who took the place of Moses. This is the same Joshua who accompanied Caleb as a spy into the promised land. Remember how he saw the possibilities? Remember how he brought back a good report? I have come to realize that being a possibilitarian requires courage and strength, two characteristics Joshua was blessed to have. "And Joshua, he shall go over before thee, as the Lord hath said. . . . And Moses called unto Joshua, and said unto him in the sight of all Israel, *Be strong and of a good courage:* for thou must go with this people unto the land which the Lord hath sworn . . . to give them; and thou shalt cause them to inherit it. And the Lord, he it is that doth go before thee; he will be with thee, he will not fail thee, neither forsake thee: fear not, neither be dismayed" (Deuteronomy 31:3, 7–8; emphasis added). Did you know that the Lord counseled Joshua to "be strong and of a good courage" six different times between Deuteronomy 31 and the first chapter of Joshua?

As we read the book of Joshua, we begin to understand why Joshua needed that counsel. It is because what he was about to do would require great strength, it would require courage, but most important, it would require him to know that the Lord would be with him wherever he went. Joshua teaches us that when you combine courage and strength with the companionship of the Lord, you can expect miracles—possibilities beyond your expectations. For it was Joshua himself who said, "To morrow the Lord will do wonders among you" (Joshua 3:5).

"Be strong and of a good courage." Why would strength and courage be good qualities for a possibilitarian?

In honor of Joshua, perhaps you could practice being a possibilitarian. Find courage. Gather strength. Allow the Lord to be with you wherever you go. Then prepare to experience wonders. "Greet each day with an enthusiastic welcome no matter how it looks. The covenant with God to which you are true enables you to become enlightened by him, and nothing is impossible for you" (F. Enzio Busche, "Unleashing the Dormant Spirit").

A Scarlet Thread

Very few women are mentioned within the accounts of the scriptures, and rarely are they mentioned by name.

For that reason I am fascinated by the story of Rahab. I find myself wondering how, in a city so filled with wickedness, she came to know the Lord.

When the two spies Joshua sent to Jericho showed up at her door, Rahab hid them, and because of her kindness she was given a promise from the spies that she would live through the destruction of Jericho. Rahab asked if that promise could be extended to "my father, and my mother, and my brethren, and my sisters" (Joshua 2:13). In order to make sure she and her family would be saved in the moment of destruction, the two spies instructed her, "Behold, when we come into the land, thou shalt bind this line of scarlet thread in the window which thou didst let us down by: and thou shalt bring thy father, and thy mother, and thy brethren, and all thy father's household. . . . And she bound the scarlet line in the window" (Joshua 2:18, 21).

In the moment when Jericho was destroyed, "Joshua saved Rahab the harlot alive, and her father's household, and all that she had; and she dwelleth in Israel even unto this day; because she hid the messengers, which Joshua sent to spy out Jericho" (Joshua 6:25).

I am drawn to the symbolism in this story. We learn of a young woman whose heart had been prepared for the moment when two messengers would knock on her door and a conversation would take place in which Rahab would come to know the Lord of Israel. Once the messengers had left, she shared that belief with her father, her mother, her brothers, and her sisters. Because she had allowed those two men entrance into her home, and through her faith, her entire family was saved. Delivered.

The scarlet thread Rahab hung in her window served as a reminder that her home was to be spared from the destruction. Passed over. Protected. I want to place a scarlet thread in my window—a reminder that just as Joshua saved Rahab, the Savior can save each member of my family.

> Could the sacrament become more of a scarlet thread in your life? How could you prepare to take His name more sincerely?

I am reminded of the sacrament—a scarlet-thread moment that allows deliverance, safety, and protection for my family. The sacrament gives us a weekly opportunity to always remember Him, to take upon us His name so that we might be saved. His name becomes the scarlet thread—a means of protection, deliverance, and safety. But to fully participate in the blessing of the Atonement, we cannot be casual observers. It is through our faith, our works, and our longing to know more of the Lord that we fully experience the blessings. The thought of this motivates me to begin preparing today for the Sabbath. In that moment of Sunday worship I do not want to be just a casual observer. I want to prepare my heart, just as Rahab did, to know more of the Lord, and to come to more fully understand how His Atonement can bless my life and the life of my family. Then taking His name will become my scarlet thread.

Leave Nothing Undone

I have a raspberry garden that requires caretaking. If I am not careful, it can be overtaken by weeds that will eventually choke out the raspberries completely.

Every spring as we begin to weed the garden, the task at hand overwhelms us. We have to pay particular attention to every single weed. None can be left behind, not even the very small ones; the job requires that nothing be left undone. So we pull out every weed one by one down to the roots, until none are left, so there is no chance of one small weed overtaking the raspberries.

The process reminds me of the description in the book of Joshua of how the people of Israel went to war against all of the cities in the promised land. "As the Lord commanded Moses his servant, so did Moses command Joshua, and so did Joshua; he *left nothing undone* of all that the Lord commanded Moses" (Joshua 11:15; emphasis added). He took all the land, and "Joshua made war *a long time* with all those kings" (Joshua 11:18; emphasis added). "The king of Jericho, one . . . the king of Jerusalem, one . . . the king of Makkedah, one" (Joshua 12: 9–10, 16). Joshua checked them off one by one as they were conquered completely—none left, so there would be no chance of Israel being overtaken. I have to be honest, I worried a little as I read these war chapters. Were the people that dangerous? Did the Israelites really have to destroy every one?

The Book of Mormon provides the answer: "And after they had crossed the river Jordan he did make them mighty unto the driving out of the children of the land, yea, unto the scattering them to destruction. And now, do ye suppose that the children of this land, who were in the land of promise, who were driven out by our fathers, do ye suppose that they were righteous? Behold, I say unto you, Nay. . . . This people had rejected every word of God, and they were ripe in iniquity; and the fulness of the wrath of God was upon them; and the Lord did curse the land against them . . . unto their destruction" (1 Nephi 17:32–33, 35).

I consider the raspberry garden and realize that sometimes a very small seed can quickly overtake a very large garden. The Lord knows this, and He knows how to protect us against small things that could eventually destroy us. The people in the land could be compared to the sins of our lives. We can't just focus on the big ones, the dangerous ones. We have to remember to work on the little ones, even the ones that seem innocent. We must keep trying to conquer them until the day they are gone.

Is there anything in your life that has been left undone? How might you go about conquering that thing?

One day we will rest from this constant battle, but now we fight. It might take a long time, but we must leave nothing undone. The conquering will make us stronger. I love the verse in Joshua 14:11–12 when Caleb says, "As yet I am as strong this day as I was in the day that Moses sent me: as my strength was then, even so is my strength now, for war, both to go out, and to come in. Now therefore give me this mountain . . . the Lord will be with me."

A Torch-Like Spirit

In the book of Judges we read about "Deborah, a prophetess, the wife of Lapidoth, she judged Israel at that time" (Judges 4:4). One Bible scholar explains that the term *wife of Lapidoth* could also have been translated in Hebrew to read "a woman of a torch-like spirit" (in Alfred Edersheim, *Bible History,* 3:121). I love his translation: *Deborah, a prophetess, a woman of torch-like spirit, she judged Israel at that time.* That is the way I want to remember Deborah, as a woman with a torch-like spirit. No wonder the children of Israel came up to be judged by her as she sat under the palm tree in Mount Ephraim. I am sure the spirit that she carried was inviting and wise. The scriptures teach that hers was also a spirit that prompted courage.

On the day that Deborah persuaded Barak to gather his army to fight against Sisera, with their nine hundred chariots of iron, Barak had only one request, "If thou wilt go with me, then I will go: but if thou wilt not go with me, then I will not go. And she said, I will surely go with thee" (Judges 4:8–9). Deborah's torch-like spirit had the power to instill courage in others and to inspire them to follow the command of the Lord. Where did this power come from? Remember, Deborah was a prophetess. The scriptures teach that "*the testimony of Jesus* is the spirit of prophecy" (Revelation 19:10; emphasis added). Perhaps Deborah's strength of spirit came from her testimony of Christ.

After the army was defeated and Israel was delivered, Deborah and Barak sang a song of praise. In Judges 5:7 one verse of this song contains a sentence that is profound, "I Deborah arose, that I arose a mother in Israel."

A mother in Israel delivered the people from bondage—a woman with a torch-like spirit, a woman with the testimony of Jesus.

Have you ever taken the time to ponder how many mothers in Israel have been a part of the process of deliverance throughout the generations of time? Mary, the mother of Jesus; Elisabeth, the mother of John the Baptist; Jochebed, the mother of Moses; Hannah, the mother of Samuel; the mothers of the stripling warriors. Sometimes we question the worth of women in the Lord's plan. The story of Deborah speaks loud and clear in this regard—never underestimate the power of a righteous woman.

> Consider how a torch-like spirit would have the power to instill courage and inspire others.

Recently I had the opportunity to visit with a group of young women. There was a sweet spirit that permeated the room; it was also a spirit of great power. I listened as a young woman stood to explain a symbol of her belief. She spoke of a logo that represents the light of Christ, inviting all to come unto Christ. In that moment I was reminded of Deborah, a woman with a torch-like spirit, and I wondered, What if each of us could become women with torch-like spirits? What if we could become inspired, wise, and courageous? What if we could lead others to follow the Lord?

Perhaps we could be a little more like Deborah, who reminds us of the mark a righteous woman can have on the darkness that surrounds us. She was a woman with a torch-like spirit, filled with the testimony of Christ.

She was a righteous mother in Israel.

Every Man in His Place

Gideon, one of God's heroes, a mighty man of valor, considered himself the least in his father's house. Was it his humility that allowed the Lord to mold him into the hero he was meant to become? The Lord promised Gideon, "Surely I will be with thee" (Judges 6:16), and Gideon asked for a sign. The asking must have come from a pure heart, with real intent, for Gideon was not punished for his questioning but rather taught. First there rose up fire out of the rock. Then Gideon and his ten servants went by night and cast down the altar of Baal without repercussion. Last, Gideon proved the Lord with the fleece of wool on the floor. Within each lesson a measure of trust was forged, until finally Gideon learned to act on the word of the Lord without question, doubt, or fear.

Once this relationship of trust was established, Gideon rose up early and prepared his army for battle. "And the Lord said unto Gideon, The people that are with thee are too many" (Judges 7:2). So Gideon began the process of selecting an army fit for the Lord. The first group asked to leave were those who were afraid. After that, ten thousand remained. Still the Lord said, "The people are yet too many; bring them down unto the water, and I will try them for thee there" (Judges 7:4). Alfred Edersheim, a Bible scholar, explains this test: "If we ask about the rationale of this means of distinction, we conclude, of course, that it indicated the bravest and most ardent warriors, who would not stoop to kneel, but hastily quenched their thirst out of the hollow of their hands, in order to hasten to battle. But Jewish tradition assigns another and deeper meaning to it. It declares that the practice of kneeling was characteristic of the service of Baal. . . . Thus the three hundred would represent those in the host of Israel—'all the knees which have not bowed unto Baal' (1 Kings 19:18)" (*Bible History,* 3:138).

Now only three hundred men remained to face the camp of Midian, 135,000 men strong. Gideon prepared his warriors for the battle. Their weaponry consisted of a trumpet, a pitcher, and a lamp. His counsel to them was clear, "Look on me, and do likewise . . . as I do, so shall ye do" (Judges 7:17). Amazingly, the men didn't question the weaponry they were given; Gideon had chosen an army that was capable of trust. Instead they focused on Gideon, one of God's heroes, a man who had come to trust the Lord—implicitly. "And they stood every man in his place" (Judges 7:21).

Have you experienced a moment when you had to put your trust in the Lord? What was it that enabled you to stand in that place?

"May we always remember this profound lesson: that we are banner bearers of the Lord Jesus Christ, upheld by the Holy Spirit of God, faithful and true to the end, each one devoted to give our all to the cause of Zion and bound by covenant to stand close together" (Dieter F. Uchtdorf, "Lift Where You Stand," 56).

whither thou goest

The end of the book of Judges is filled with wickedness. There are images I don't want to think about, experiences that make me question why it is so hard to remember God, to look to Him, to follow Him. Is it so hard to do the right thing? In the midst of all that is unsettled about Israel in the end of the book of Judges, we might find ourselves questioning, *Wasn't there anyone who knew what it was to be true?*

Then we turn the page and discover the book of Ruth.

Ruth was a woman of virtue in the midst of gross wickedness. I can't help but wonder, Does a righteous woman today stand out in the way the book of Ruth stands out after the book of Judges? I won't tell you her whole story, I will let you turn to the scriptures—for it is a very pleasant read. But I would like to share some of the verses I love most, which contain my favorite descriptions of Ruth:

"And Ruth said, Intreat me not to leave thee, or to return from following after thee: for whither thou goest, I will go; and where thou lodgest, I will lodge: thy people shall be my people, and thy God my God" (Ruth 1:16–17).

"She was stedfastly minded" (Ruth 1:18).

"It hath fully been shewed me, all that thou hast done unto thy mother in law" (Ruth 2:11).

"Blessed be thou of the Lord, my daughter: for thou hast shewed more kindness in the latter end than at the beginning" (Ruth 3:10).

"For all the city of my people doth know that thou art a virtuous woman" (Ruth 3:11).

The characteristics of a truly righteous woman can be found within the story of Ruth. She was a woman of loyalty who came to know the Lord. Ruth had a steadfast mind. She was kind, virtuous, and true. The verses speak of a remarkable woman. My favorite verse about Ruth is found in the middle of chapter two, "The Lord recompense thy work, and a *full reward* be given thee of the Lord God of Israel, under whose wings thou art come to trust" (Ruth 2:12; emphasis added).

> What does Doctrine and Covenants 29:2 teach about the principle of trusting the Lord enough to find shelter under His wing?

I know what it is to look to the Lord with a heart full of hope, when it seems as if hope is gone. I know what it is to give, and give, and give, and expect nothing in return. I know what it is to love so deeply that loyalty isn't a decision but rather a consequence of that love. And I know, even though I don't understand it, how it is to come to trust the Lord even when I am being led down an unfamiliar path that I would not have chosen.

I want to learn from Ruth.

On those days when true love leads to greatest loyalty, when my heart is exhausted from giving, when I wonder if the path I tread will ever lead to a promised land, when it seems that hope is gone, I hope that my prayer might echo that of Ruth. May every moment of my life lead me to know the Lord God of Israel, under whose wings I too can come to trust.

"Thou seekest to destroy . . . a mother in Israel: why . . . ?"

2 Samuel 20:19

Invitations from

The First Book of Samuel, The Second Book of Samuel, The First Book of the Kings, and The Second Book of the Kings

Some Blessings Come Late

When Hannah approached the Lord, the scriptures tell us it was out of an abundance of grief. Her overwhelming sadness is described as a bitterness of soul. She wept sore, prayed, and did not eat as she prepared to petition the Lord. Finally, after all her preparation—and after many years of waiting—Hannah prayed for the blessing of a child, promising that she would give that child to the Lord all the days of his life.

In her abundance of grief, Hannah pled with the Lord, and He answered through His prophet, "Go in peace: and the God of Israel grant thee thy petition that thou hast asked of him" (1 Samuel 1:17). I love to think of Hannah walking out of the temple that day. The scriptures tell us that she "went her way, and did eat, and her countenance was no more sad" (1 Samuel 1:18). This is not a description of what doubt looks like, it is what faith looks like, even after years of praying and hoping and petitioning for the same blessing over and over again.

After Hannah petitioned the Lord, the scriptures tell us, "the Lord remembered her" (1 Samuel 1:19). Every time I read this sentence, my testimony of God's love is increased. I know that because He remembered Hannah in her abundance of grief, He will remember me in mine. I know not when the blessing will come, but I know I will not be forgotten of the Lord. Elder Jeffrey R. Holland promised, "Some blessings come soon, some come late, and some don't come until heaven; but for those who embrace the gospel of Jesus Christ, *they come*" ("'An High Priest of Good Things to Come,'" 38; emphasis in original). Finally, Hannah gave birth to a son, "and called his name Samuel, saying, because I have asked him of the Lord" (1 Samuel 1:20).

When Samuel was very young, his mother took him to Eli, the prophet, and lent him to the Lord as she had promised. "And she said, O my lord, as thy soul liveth, my lord, I am the woman that stood by thee here, praying unto the Lord. For this child I prayed; and the Lord hath given me my petition which I asked of him" (1 Samuel 1:26–27).

For this child I prayed. I can't imagine how hard it must have been to entrust the tiny child she had longed for into the hands of someone else to be raised—to give up the blessing she had yearned for after having him for such a short time. But the story does not speak of sadness; instead Hannah bears testimony of the goodness of God, saying, "My heart rejoiceth in the Lord. . . . There is none holy as the Lord: for there is none beside thee: neither is there any rock like our God" (1 Samuel 2:1–2). Through the waiting, the grief, the bitterness, the tears, the petitioning, and even through the blessing, Hannah had come to know the Lord. Perhaps Samuel, this gift from the Lord, might be labeled as a blessing come late. But have you ever considered that the answer to her prayer that day in the temple might not have been the greatest blessing Hannah received? Maybe, after all, Hannah's greatest blessing was what came as a result of the waiting, the petitioning, the grief—because through the process the Savior had become her rock. Could that have been the greater blessing?

In the years that followed, even though Samuel was not with her, Hannah remembered her precious gift from the Lord. She spent countless hours sewing for her son. Once every year she visited the beloved child that she had pled for and brought him what must surely have been a token of her love—a handmade little coat. The scripture tells us, "Moreover his mother made him a little coat, and brought it to him from year to year" (1 Samuel 2:19). Right away we know how important each of those little coats must have been to Samuel. If they hadn't been, he wouldn't have remembered to write them into the history of his life. I am confident that Samuel wore each of those coats and thought of his mother, whose prayers had resulted in the miracle of his life. He must have known that while wearing those coats he was wrapped up in her love. Perhaps the coats became something to remember her by.

When you pour out your soul to the Lord, what is it you petition for right now? Is there something you could learn from Hannah's experience that might help your situation?

Have you ever had a Hannah moment, a situation when you experienced an abundance of grief or a bitterness of soul? Can you think of a time when you have wept sore? Have you ever poured out your soul to the Lord? Hannah's story is a tender reminder that the Lord does hear and answer our prayers. The entry on prayer in the Bible Dictionary is also a great resource for understanding prayer.

When you find yourself begging the Lord for the blessings you stand in need of, perhaps you could remember this promise found in Hannah's story: "He raiseth up the poor . . . and lifteth up the beggar from the dunghill, to set them among princes, and to make them inherit the throne of glory" (1 Samuel 2:8). The Lord knows how to raise our spirits and lift our hearts.

His promises are sure.
His blessing will come.

Here I Raise My Ebenezer

Almost twenty-five years ago I was asked to play the piano at a missionary homecoming. The song was one I had never heard before. It was titled "Come, Thou Fount of Every Blessing." The missionary's sister had been asked to sing. I hate to admit it, but some of the words just didn't make sense to us, particularly the phrase, "Here I raise my Ebenezer; Here by Thy great help I've come." We had no idea who Ebenezer was, and we figured no one else in the congregation would either, so we decided to change that part of the song, and we left out the line entirely.

After the homecoming, the missionary approached us to thank us. "But," he said, "you left out my very favorite part of the song." We told him that since we didn't know who Ebenezer was, the line didn't make sense to us. Then we asked him what the meaning was. With a smile, he told us we would have to figure it out for ourselves, and hinted that the answer could be found in the scriptures. I searched the Bible Dictionary and found the answer in the seventh chapter of 1 Samuel.

Just as each of the prophets had done before him, there came a moment in Samuel's life when he asked Israel to put away their strange gods and turn to the Lord. This time it was so that they could be delivered from the Philistines. Samuel asked them to "prepare your hearts unto the Lord, and serve him only: and he will deliver you. . . . Gather all

Israel . . . and I will pray for you unto the Lord. And they gathered together . . . and fasted on that day" (1 Samuel 7:3, 5–6). Israel was afraid, and they said to Samuel, "Cease not to cry unto the Lord our God for us, that he will save us. . . . And Samuel cried unto the Lord for Israel; and the Lord heard him" (1 Samuel 7:8–9).

Israel prevailed. "Then Samuel took a stone, and called the name of it Eben-ezer, saying, Hitherto hath the Lord helped us" (1 Samuel 7:12). If you look at the footnote for *Eben-ezer* in verse 12, you will find that the name means "the stone of help." *Here I raise my Ebenezer; here by Thy great help I've come.* The stone became a memorial for Israel of a time when the Lord had helped them through a situation they could not have made it through on their own.

Do you have an Ebenezer? What is it?

Do you have an Ebenezer? It might not be a stone. Anything that physically reminds you of a time when you felt the help of the Lord could count. Mine is a small woven basket with blue fabric nestled inside. I bought it sixteen years ago during one of the hardest times of my life. It was a time I really wasn't sure I would make it through. I was afraid, exhausted, and spent. I felt that I wasn't physically or emotionally up to the challenge placed before me.

During that time I found great counsel in a blessing I was given, "Have an optimistic approach to the life that is yours." Right then, in that moment, I wasn't really enthusiastic about the life that was mine. I laughed out loud at the thought of having an optimistic approach to a situation that had filled my entire world with darkness.

But I trusted the advice from the Lord. So I spent a long time thinking about how I could be more optimistic about the situation I was in. I needed to find a constant reminder that would help me remember to have optimism. I knew the Lord would help me live up to that counsel if I prepared my heart to follow His words.

So I bought a happy basket.

The situation I was in was not happy. But the basket was. Every single time I looked at it, I remembered the Lord. And somehow the Lord helped me through. In fact, most often what got me through the darkest days was knowing that the night would come, and with it the opportunity I would have to turn to the Lord in prayer. Sometimes those prayers lasted most of the night. I look back at that time and know that I would not have made it through if it hadn't been for Him.

Now when I see that basket I think to myself, "Hitherto hath the Lord helped us." I don't need the basket anymore. But I will never give it away. It has become for me a memory of a time of great need when I received help from the Lord. Strength beyond my own. Deliverance.

As hard as it was, it is a time I never want to forget.

To the Rescue

Have you ever experienced a riptide? This type of tide can be extremely dangerous. The current is so powerful it can drag a swimmer standing waist-deep out into deeper waters and the swimmer can die from the exhaustion of trying to swim back to shore. So a lifeguard is placed on duty. A lifesaver. A rescuer. Sometimes there are two. Their vigil is constant. Always they are watching for signs of danger, listening for a cry for help, ready in an instant to pursue. Their goal is to recover all.

When the Amalekites invaded, they took the women and children captive, both great and small. The people wept and lifted up their voices. "And David was greatly distressed . . . but David encouraged himself in the Lord his God" (1 Samuel 30:6). And he enquired after the Lord, "Shall I pursue?" And the Lord answered, "Pursue: for thou shalt . . . without fail recover all" (1 Samuel 30:8). So David went to the rescue. Along the way he found an Egyptian in the field and asked, "To whom belongest thou?" (1 Samuel 30:13). After discovering that the man was a servant to an Amalekite, David asked if he would be willing to join their cause. The servant agreed as long as David would not return him to the man who held him captive.

As the Israelites approached the Amalekites, they discovered they were "spread abroad upon all the earth" (1 Samuel 30:16). But still

David pressed forward and led the rescue. "And David recovered all that the Amalekites had carried away . . . and there was nothing lacking to them, neither small nor great, neither sons nor daughters, neither spoil, nor any thing that they had taken to them: David recovered all" (1 Samuel 30:18–19). The wives. The children. The small. The great. Even the servant in the field. *David recovered all.*

David is often spoken of as a type of Christ. Within this story we see that type. In David we see a reminder of the Savior—a lifeguard, a lifesaver, a rescuer. One whose vigil is constant. Always He is listening. Always He hears the cry for help. His arms are outstretched constantly. He has promised to recover us, every one. To recover all.

How might you assist in the rescue?

Sometimes His rescuing effort requires our help. Today I hold in my mind an image of two young men, dressed in well-worn suits, white shirts, and ties. Each wears a name tag over his heart with the Lord's name written in bold just below his. They are acting as His lifeguards, His lifesavers, His rescuers. I pray for them, these rescuers all over the world, the servants in the field. May they rescue those who are seeking and lead them to the Lord.

"In a very real sense, those persons stranded . . . in the storm-tossed sea are like many . . . who await rescue. . . . Their hearts yearn for help. Mothers and fathers pray. . . . Wives and children plead. . . . I pray that all of us . . . may sense our responsibilities and, as one, follow our Leader—even the Lord Jesus Christ . . . to the rescue" (Thomas S. Monson, "To the Rescue," 50).

A Mother in Israel

When I read about the wise woman in 2 Samuel 20, I can't help but admire her courage. As Joab and his army approached the city, I wonder if all of the people took refuge inside their homes. I picture this old and frail woman walking out of the city walls to meet Joab, who was armed for battle and intent on destroying the entire city in his pursuit of Sheba. I can imagine her saying, "Hear, hear; say, I pray you . . . Come near hither, that I may speak with thee" (2 Samuel 20:16). I picture Joab bending close, perhaps out of respect, to hear what the wise woman would say. I love the way she introduced herself to him, "I am one of them that are peaceable and faithful in Israel" (2 Samuel 20:19). She does not give her name, she gives a description that inspires honor and admiration. Then she speaks a line that captures my interest, "Thou seekest to destroy . . . a mother in Israel: why . . . ?" (2 Samuel 20:19).

I think of the wise women I admire most in my life, handmaids, peaceable and faithful mothers in Israel. Then I think of the world we live in, filled with evil designs of people bent on destroying all that is peaceable, faithful, honorable. I hear that same echo, "Thou seekest to destroy . . . a mother in Israel: why . . . ?" I know that if Satan can destroy a mother, he can destroy an entire generation. So I look to see how *this* wise woman out of the city, this mother in Israel, will respond to the danger she has been placed in. I want to learn from her example.

Joab explains to her that it is not his desire to destroy the mothers and all they hold dear to them, but that there is an evil man within the walls of the city who "hath lifted up his hand against the king" (2 Samuel 20:21). He must be delivered out of the city in order for the mothers and the city to be saved. "Then the woman went unto all the people in her wisdom. And they cut off the head of Sheba the son of Bichri, and cast it out to Joab. And he blew a trumpet, and . . . retired from the city" (2 Samuel 20:22).

The answer this wise woman teaches is that together we must be watchful. We cannot allow that which is evil or threatens our belief to find a haven within our homes or within our hearts. It must be cast out for us to remain safe. Her story is a gentle reminder of our responsibility as mothers and the important role that we fulfill on a daily basis.

I want to be a mother in Israel just like this wise woman was, peaceable and faithful, strong in my belief, courageous enough to stand up and protect all that I love, willing to cast out that which could bring us harm. As I prepare a place in my home for scripture study, for family home evening, for family prayer, I wonder if perhaps, in that moment, I am following her example, "Hear, hear; say, I pray you . . . Come near hither, that I may speak with thee."

Perhaps I too can stand up for and protect that which is most dear to me.

"Will you rise to the challenge of being mothers in these perilous times, though doing so may test the last ounce of your endurance and courage and faith? Will you stand steadfast and immovable as a mother in israel?"

(Sheri Dew, "Are We Not All Mothers?" 98).

That which Doth Cost Me Nothing

Most mornings, just as the sun begins to rise, my daughter Grace and I drive toward the light peeking over the mountains. Our course is constant, familiar, and every day we pass the same house—it is the house where we learn to walk in the commandments of the Lord, the house where the Lord dwells. Just seeing it has the power to lift my heart, to direct my focus, to inspire my soul. Sometimes I wonder who built that house. I thought about it again as I read the verses that describe the building of Solomon's temple.

Several lessons on sacrifice can be learned from this chapter in 2 Samuel. Three have particular significance to me. The first lesson is found in 2 Samuel 24, when King David approached Araunah to buy the land for the temple and Araunah offered to give it to him. But David turned away the gift, saying, "Nay; but I will surely buy it of thee at a price: *neither will I offer burnt offerings unto the Lord my God of that which doth cost me nothing*" (2 Samuel 24:24; emphasis added).

I can't help but ponder what David was teaching. His offering to build the house of the Lord would come at a price. It was important to him that it would cost something. I wonder if the same is true of my temple worship. What price is it worth to me? I cannot be content with an offering "which doth cost me nothing," whether it is time, convenience, or obedience. The cost, or the sacrifice, is part of what makes the offering sincere. Sacred.

The second lesson is found within the chapters on building. I am intrigued by the thought of those who bore burdens and the hewers up in the mountains. I can picture them, these hewers and these stone squarers, as they bore the burden of each of the stones that made up the temple walls. "And they brought great stones, costly stones, and hewed stones, to lay the foundation of the house" (1 Kings 5:17). I think of these stones and am reminded of a quotation from J. Golden Kimball with reference to the Salt Lake Temple: "When I think about that building, every stone in it is a sermon to me. It tells of suffering, it tells of sacrifice, it preaches—every rock in it, preaches a discourse" (in Taylor, *J. Golden Kimball,* 155). Again I am reminded of the sacrifice required of those who want to worship within a house of God.

What is the difference between a sacrifice that costs something as opposed to that which doth cost nothing?

Last, the doors that entered into the Holy of Holies were made of olive trees. One had to pass through the olive trees to enter the presence of God. Olive trees are symbolic of Christ. It is what happened beneath the olive trees that I am reminded of now—the symbolism reflects the sacrifice.

There is a promise that comes with this cost, this sacrifice, this offering: "Concerning this house which thou art in building, if thou wilt walk in my statutes, and execute my judgments, and keep all my commandments to walk in them; then will I perform my word with thee . . . and I will dwell among the children of Israel, and will not forsake my people Israel" (1 Kings 6:12–13).

It is a promise worth the sacrifice.

Come Running

The story of the widow of Zarephath teaches about the blessings that come when we drop everything and come running.

You remember that the land of Israel was suffering from a famine. Elijah had been fed by ravens near the brook Cherith, but eventually even that brook ran dry, so the Lord spoke to Elijah and told him to go to Zarephath to dwell. The Lord had commanded a widow there to sustain the prophet.

We do not know much about the widow, but this much we do know—her cupboard was bare and her situation was dire. Why would the Lord choose her to sustain Elijah? Through the asking, was the Lord preparing a way to bless her? Would her obedience and her sacrifice bring forth blessings that would not fail?

I love that when Elijah came to the gate of the city, "behold, the widow woman was there" (1 Kings 17:10). She was in the place where the Lord needed her to be in the moment He needed her to be there. The prophet asked, "Fetch me, I pray thee, a little water in a vessel, that I may drink" (1 Kings 17:10).

Notice what happens next—it is on her way to fulfill the first command that he asks of her the second. "And *as she was going* to fetch it, he called to her, and said, Bring me, I pray thee, a morsel of bread in thine hand" (1 Kings 17:11; emphasis added). The first request would require great effort, as they were in a famine. The second request would require great sacrifice because her cupboard was already bare.

In this moment the woman poured out her soul to the prophet, explaining her dire situation. His answer was filled with hope: "Fear not . . . for thus saith the Lord God of Israel, The barrel of meal shall not waste, neither shall the cruse of oil fail, until the day that the Lord sendeth rain upon the earth. And she went and did" (1 Kings 17:13–15).

Several key phrases in this story testify of this woman's willingness to serve: She was there. She was going. She went and did. This willingness to serve and to obey led to great blessings in her behalf.

Elder Jeffrey R. Holland tells of a story that took place amidst the terrible hostilities against the early Latter-day Saints in Missouri. Brother James Hendricks had been shot by mobbers in what has become known as the Battle of Crooked River. He and his wife, Drusilla, had been forced to flee with their family and were living in a dugout—a primitive shelter scooped out of the hillside—in Quincy, Illinois. James was an invalid now, and his family soon found themselves in dire circumstances:

"Within two weeks the Hendrickses were on the verge of starvation, having only one spoonful of sugar and a saucerful of cornmeal remaining in their possession. In the great tradition of LDS women, Drusilla made mush out of it for James and the children, thus stretching its contents as far as she could make it go. When that small offering was consumed by her famished family, she washed everything, cleaned their little dugout as thoroughly as she could, and quietly waited to die.

"Not long thereafter the sound of a wagon brought Drusilla to her feet. It was their neighbor Reuben Allred. He said he had a feeling they were out of food, so on his way into town he'd had a sack of grain ground into meal for them.

"Shortly thereafter Alexander Williams arrived with two bushels of meal on his shoulder. He told Drusilla that he'd been extremely busy but the Spirit had whispered to him that 'Brother Hendricks' family is suffering, so I dropped everything and came [running].'

"May God, who has blessed all of us so mercifully and many of us so abundantly, bless us with one thing more. May he bless us to hear the often silent cries of the sorrowing and the afflicted, the downtrodden, the disadvantaged, the poor. Indeed may he bless us to hear the whispering of the Holy Spirit when any neighbor anywhere 'is suffering,' and to 'drop everything and come running'" ("A Handful of Meal and a Little Oil," 31).

When have you experienced a moment of true charity, when someone came running in your behalf?

These two stories speak of the very essence of charity. Life has taught me that often the truest charity comes at the cost of greatest sacrifice. The widow of Zarephath with her cruse of oil and her barrel of meal is a humble example of this great truth.

As I have pondered the cruse of oil that would not fail, I can't help but think of my husband, my father, our home teachers, my brothers, my sons, and the men who live in my neighborhood. These are men who, in response to a fervent call day or night, come running, bearing the priesthood, blessing my family.

A cruse of oil that will not fail.

When I think of the meal that shall not waste, I can't help but picture the women in my neighborhood. Often, in the late afternoon, you will see them knocking on the door of a family in need. Their arms are full. They come bearing fruit, bread, dinner, and dessert.

A meal that shall not waste.

These are images of the true charity that comes at the cost of great sacrifice. Might we each learn from this humble widow to open our eyes to see the suffering, even in the midst of our own trials. And may we "go and do" as she "went and did" (1 Kings 17:13, 15), even if it means that we drop everything and come running.

They That Be with Us

Have you ever had one of those moments when you are doing your best, giving your all, trying to make a difference, and yet it seems like the world is conspiring against you? In those moments, even when we are on the Lord's errand, perhaps we feel twinges of doubt—enough doubt that even our hearts fail us. Where is it that we look for hope? For the courage to press forward? For the strength to go on?

I love the lesson we are taught in 2 Kings 6 as the king of Syria warred against Israel. My imagination contrives a constant battle. Ongoing. Tiring. I have known moments like that, when it seems someone has a constant agenda to fight against all that I am trying to accomplish.

In this case, the prophet Elisha was on Israel's side. True to his calling, he sent direction and warning; his counsel was given as protection. The king of Israel followed Elisha's advice and his life was spared "not once nor twice" (2 Kings 6:10). We are led to believe that his life was spared every time he followed the counsel of the prophet. I believe the same is true today.

It didn't take long before the king of Syria became frustrated. He wondered if there was a spy in his camp. One of his servants pointed out that the prophet Elisha was the one getting in the way of his plan to destroy Israel. So the king decided to capture Elisha. After discovering that

Elisha was in Doran, the king sent "horses, and chariots, and a great host: and they came by night, and compassed the city about" (2 Kings 6:14).

I can imagine the servant of the prophet Elisha rising early that next morning. I picture him preparing for the journey ahead. As he went about gathering supplies for the trek to Samaria, I can understand the worry that must have filled his heart when he discovered that the city was encompassed round about by the great host. I can almost hear the fear in his voice as he approached Elisha, "Alas, my master! how shall we do?" (2 Kings 6:15). It becomes real to me because I have felt that worry, that sense of imminent defeat, the fear that I am not enough to face the task in front of me. There have been times in my life when my purpose seems to be threatened by what appears to be an enemy much stronger and more organized than I am. I love what happened in this crucial moment. Elisha replied with confidence, "Fear not: for they that be with us are more than they that be with them" (2 Kings 6:16).

And then he prayed.

He asked the Lord to bless his servant, to "open his eyes, that he may see" (2 Kings 6:17). So the Lord opened the eyes of the servant, and he beheld that the mountain was full of horses and chariots of fire—heaven's help.

Within this story we are taught a principle that we must never forget. The unseen presence of God and of His help is real. If our eyes could be opened to see, we would realize that we do not ever wage a battle for righteousness alone. The Lord is with us; heavenly help attends us. This knowledge alone should give us all the encouragement we need to move forward.

With the help of the Lord, Elisha and his servant were able to make it safely to Samaria, leading the entire Syrian army captive behind them. Safely protected by the Lord, they accomplished an unbelievable feat without weapons, without even the help of an army—simply with the assistance of the Lord. Heaven's help.

I love the condition of Elisha's heart at the end of this remarkable journey. The king of Israel asked Elisha when he saw him, "Shall I smite them? shall I smite them? And he answered, Thou shalt not smite them: . . . set bread and water before them, that they may eat and drink, and go to their master" (2 Kings 6:21–22).

> Can you remember a moment in your life when you have relied on heaven's help?

I wonder if my heart is in the same place. It seems like perhaps my heart would not be so kind. There have been those who have tried to frustrate my purpose, who have caused me to doubt, who have fought against what is in my heart. My first inclination seems to lean toward revenge or retribution. My first instinct is not always kindness or compassion. Perhaps it is heaven's help that I must turn to in these moments, also. Maybe, once again, I need to pray to the Lord that He might open my eyes to see.

Heaven's help is real. We must learn to trust the unseen, to rely on the certain presence of God's help even when our mortal eyes can't comprehend it. Those who trust in the reality of heaven's help can accomplish great things. They become Saints who press forward with faith in every footstep. That is where they find hope, courage, strength to go on. It is the faith that is built upon the reality of heaven's help . . . they that be with us.

A Great Woman

"Is thine heart right, as my heart is with thy heart?" (2 Kings 10:15). What does it mean for a heart to be *right?*

I am reminded of one of my favorite stories found in 2 Kings 4. It is about a woman whose name we are never told. She is known simply as a great woman—a woman whose heart was right.

Elisha was a prophet of the Lord. Every time he visited the city Shunem, he would pass by the home of a great woman who would offer him bread. One day this great woman said to her husband, "Behold now, I perceive that this is a holy man of God, which passeth by us continually" (2 Kings 4:9). Right away we learn two things about this woman. First, she knew that Elisha was a holy man, and second, we learn that he came to her house continually.

From this great woman we learn two important lessons: We must learn to recognize the prophet today as a holy man *and* we must invite him into our house continually. Now, most likely the prophet will not visit our home today. But when we listen to general conference or read his words in the Church magazines, he is visiting our home, just as Elisha visited the woman in this story.

One day the woman asked her husband if they could make a place for the prophet to stay—a little chamber with a bed, a table, a stool, and a candlestick. Note that what this woman offered did not require a lot of money, time, or great talent. She simply offered what she had. So the prophet Elisha came and stayed in this chamber. One day, out of gratitude, he called for the woman to come to him and said, "Thou hast been careful for us with all this care; what is to be done for thee?" He wondered if he should say good things about her to the king or to the captain of the host. But the woman answered, "I dwell among mine own people" (2 Kings 4:13). Or in other words, *I am happy just the way things are and I don't expect anything in return for my service.* In our day Elisha might have asked, "What can I do to repay you?" And the woman would have answered, "Nothing." This woman was happy to serve without a reward.

Is there a way you might serve those whose paths cross yours? Has the Lord blessed you with something that would allow you to touch their hearts with your heart?

I find it fitting that her quiet act of kindness remains secret today. We know her story, but we are never told her name. She is known simply as "a great woman."

Think about the people within your circle of influence, those who walk past you every day. Is there something you could offer them? Can you think of a way you might serve them? Has the Lord blessed you with something that would allow you to touch their hearts with your heart?

Did you notice this great woman was not asked to perform that service? She wasn't given an assignment. Her actions for good were not extended because of a calling she held. She simply saw a need and filled it with her heart. That is the mark of a great woman.

I Will Heal Thee

Hezekiah's story is one of my favorite stories in the entire Bible. It brings comfort. It testifies of prayer. It speaks of hope. To fully understand the magnitude of Hezekiah's experience, we first have to come to know Hezekiah. The scriptures teach us that "he did that which was right in the sight of the Lord. . . . He trusted in the Lord God of Israel; so that after him was none like him among all the kings of Judah, nor any that were before him. For he clave to the Lord, and departed not from following him, but kept his commandments. . . . And the Lord was with him" (2 Kings 18:3, 5–7).

On one occasion it seemed that all was conspiring against Hezekiah. I am intrigued by the questions that were asked of him by those who didn't share his beliefs: "What confidence is this wherein thou trustest? . . . Now on whom dost thou trust?" (2 Kings 18:19–20). Eventually those questions prompted a letter filled with threats and deceit toward Hezekiah and his people. In this moment I love what King Hezekiah did. He went up into the house of the Lord and spread the letter before the Lord. Then he prayed. He asked the Lord for a blessing that his people would be saved, "that all the kingdoms of the earth may know that thou art the Lord God, even thou only" (2 Kings 19:19). The Lord's prophet, Isaiah, sent to Hezekiah, saying, "Thus saith the Lord God of Israel, That which thou hast prayed . . . I have heard" (2 Kings 19:20). In that moment Hezekiah learned that he could lay out his problem before the Lord and he would be heard.

I believe this experience and conversation with the Lord prepared Hezekiah's heart for a future trial. The scriptures tell us, "In those days was Hezekiah sick unto death" (2 Kings 20:1). The chapter explains that he had a wound, one that wouldn't heal. Isaiah came to Hezekiah and told him that he needed to set his house in order, for he was going to die. Hezekiah turned his face to the wall and wept sore. He prayed, "I beseech thee, O Lord, remember now how I have walked before thee in truth and with a perfect heart, and have done that which is good in thy sight" (2 Kings 20:3). Before Isaiah had even left the middle court, the voice of the Lord came to him saying, "Turn again, and tell Hezekiah . . . Thus saith the Lord . . . I have heard thy prayer, I have seen thy tears: *behold, I will heal thee* . . . and I will add unto thy days . . . and I will deliver thee . . . and I will defend this city" (2 Kings 20:5–6; emphasis added).

My thoughts turn to healing, and to the power of prayer, because I have experienced the dark moments of life, the times that cause you to turn your face to the wall, the days that invoke you to weep sore. Sometimes those moments even come after we have walked in truth, with a perfect heart—even when we are doing that which is good. Sometimes we are left with a heart that is broken. In those moments we, like Hezekiah, are in need of healing. Because the wound is so deep, it is the kind of healing that can come only from the Lord—through prayer. "O Lord, remember . . ." *Remember me.*

The story of Hezekiah teaches that we are not forgotten of the Lord, even when the trials of life seem to destroy us—especially in the moments when others might ask, "What confidence is this wherein thou trustest? . . . Now on whom dost thou trust?" In those moments, weeping sore, we must turn to the Lord—and pray. "Prayer is the act by which the will of the Father and the will of the child are brought into correspondence with each other. The object of prayer is not to change the will of God, but to secure for ourselves and for others blessings that God is already willing to grant, but that are made conditional on our asking for them. Blessings require some work or effort on our part before we can obtain them. Prayer . . . is an appointed means for obtaining the highest of all blessings" (Bible Dictionary, s.v. "Prayer").

Are you in need of healing? What can you learn from the story of Hezekiah that might help you?

Life has taught me that healing comes in many ways. Sometimes healing means saving a life, or curing an illness. Sometimes. But sometimes the illness lingers. Sometimes the life isn't saved. Even then, especially then, healing is required. As our wounded hearts cause us to turn our faces to the wall, to weep sore, hopefully they will also lead us to call on the Lord through prayer. The healing of life's deepest wounds can come only through Him. It is that kind of healing that causes us to testify, I know "that thou art the Lord God, *even thou only.*"

In moments of deepest hurt we must cleave to the Lord and remember the words the Lord's prophet, Isaiah, sent to Hezekiah: "Thus saith the Lord God of Israel, That which thou hast prayed . . . I have heard. . . . I have heard thy prayer, I have seen thy tears: behold, I will heal thee" (2 Kings 19:20; 20:5).

"There are good things found in thee,
in that thou . . . hast prepared thine heart to seek God."

2 CHRONICLES 19:3

Invitations from

The First Book of the Chronicles, The Second Book of the Chronicles, The Book of Nehemiah, The Book of Esther, and The Book of Job

Men of Valor

Over the weekend I attended a lacrosse game. This is serious business. The athletes gather with one purpose in mind: victory. They have prepared for this moment—not the kind of preparing that takes place in one afternoon, but the sort that goes on day after day, week after week, month after month. Some of these kids eat, drink, and sleep with lacrosse sticks in their hands. They are not just good at the sport, they are the elite. The varsity squad. What sets them apart is their dedication, their diligence, and their determination.

My sons have taught me that the best of the best have something in common: They have a right-hand *and* a left-hand shot. You are not born with that kind of talent. You earn it through many hours and days of practice. These boys have shot at a goal until the last light of sun faded behind the mountain; they have worked their shot until their arm muscles became so sore they could barely even lift the stick; they have emptied a bucket of balls shooting at the goal, then gathered them back up from all across the field, and then emptied the bucket again, and again, and again. They have practiced and prepared over and over and over. That's the mark of a varsity player.

When I think of these boys, I am reminded of the army that gathered to David's side as told of in the book of Chronicles.

They were mighty men of valor, heaven sent, and heaven prepared.

These men had prepared to be part of this great army day after day, week after week, month after month. They were men of might fit for the battle. They were described as men "whose faces were like the faces of lions," men who were "as swift as the roes upon the mountains" (1 Chronicles 12:8–9). These were the elite from every tribe of Israel. What set them apart was their dedication, their diligence, and their determination. "They were among the mighty men, helpers of the war. They were armed with bows, *and could use both the right hand and the left* in hurling stones and shooting arrows out of a bow" (1 Chronicles 12:1–2; emphasis added). I can't help but wonder if these men shot their arrows until the last light of sun faded behind the mountain, if they hurled stones until their arm muscles became so sore they could barely even lift them, again, and again, and again. I love what these men said to David as they came to fortify his army, "Thine are we, David, and on thy side" (1 Chronicles 12:18). They came, day by day, until the army was a great host—like the host of God. Mighty men of valor. "They were not of double heart. . . . All these men of war . . . came with a perfect heart . . . and all . . . were of one heart" (1 Chronicles 12:33, 38).

Now a different picture fills my mind—mighty men and women of valor who have prepared for this moment day after day, week after week, month after month. They have grown a foot or two, and now they are ready to teach, and preach, and live as missionaries. What sets them apart is their dedication, their diligence, and their determination. They come to fortify the Lord's army with a name tag over their hearts and angels on their right hand and on their left. Every time I see a missionary companionship I love to look at their shoes—they are always worn through. I can't help but wonder where those shoes have traveled. A worn pair of shoes tells me that those missionaries have walked until the last light of sun faded behind the mountain; they have shared their testimonies, and their time, and their love of the Lord; they have knocked on door after door, just one more door, just this one—again, and again, and again. They give their hearts day by day, week by week, month by month. These men and women of valor are witnesses of Christ, part of His army, part of a great host—the host of God.

How can you assist in strengthening the army of the Lord? Do you know a young man or a young woman who could use some encouragement from you?

David consulted with the captains and said, "If it seem good unto you, and that it be of the Lord our God, let us send abroad unto our brethren every where . . . that they may gather themselves unto us" (1 Chronicles 13:2). I think of the young men and women I know, both on the lacrosse field and off, in my neighborhood and in my school. I wonder what I might do to help them prepare for their own missions. Could I encourage them to become more fit for the battle? Might I commend them more often on their diligence, their dedication, or their determination? Today I honor those who have joined the ranks of the Lord's army, and those who will, as they sacrifice all in an effort to say, "Thine are we . . . and on thy side" (1 Chronicles 12:18).

There Are Good Things Found in Thee

The scriptures tell us that Jehoshaphat was a good man. He strengthened himself against the ways and the doings of the world, and he walked in the way his father had taught him. Because of his righteousness, great blessings came to Jehoshaphat, "and he had riches and honour in abundance. And his heart was lifted up in the ways of the Lord. . . . And Jehoshaphat waxed great exceedingly; and he built in Judah castles . . . and the men of war, mighty men of valour, were in Jerusalem" (2 Chronicles 17:5–6, 12–13).

At one point Jehoshaphat, king of Judah, joined with Ahab, king of Israel, to fight Syria. This was not a wise decision on Jehoshaphat's part, for King Ahab was a wicked man, a man who hated the Lord. Jehoshaphat didn't ask the Lord; instead he made the decision to join Ahab alone. Recognizing his mistake at the last minute, when they were beyond the point of no return, Jehoshaphat asked King Ahab to inquire of his prophets whether they should go to battle. Ahab's prophets gathered, but they did not listen to the Lord. They foretold victory. "But Jehoshaphat said, Is there not here *a prophet of the Lord* besides, that we might enquire of him? And the king of Israel said unto Jehoshaphat, There is yet one man, by whom we may enquire of the Lord: *but I hate him;* for he never prophesied good unto me, but always evil" (2 Chronicles 18:6–7; emphasis added).

Have you heard this sentiment before? Ahab didn't like what the prophet of the Lord had to say. It bothered him so much that he had grown to hate the prophet. However, because he knew he needed Jehoshaphat and his army, King Ahab called for Micaiah, the prophet. Then, Jehoshaphat and Ahab sat together on their thrones and waited to hear what Micaiah would say.

When the messenger went to get Micaiah, he said to him, "Behold, the words of the prophets declare good to the king with one assent; let thy word therefore, *I pray thee,* be like one of theirs, and speak thou good" (2 Chronicles 18:12; emphasis added). I am sure this messenger was looking out for Micaiah as he begged him to simply say exactly what everyone else was saying. But Micaiah said, "As the Lord liveth, even what my God saith, that will I speak" (2 Chronicles 18:13). When Micaiah arrived at the throne room he prophesied that Ahab would die.

Immediately Ahab turned to Jehoshaphat and said, "Did I not tell thee that he would not prophesy good unto me, but evil?" (2 Chronicles 18:17). Ahab was angry. He commanded that Micaiah be put in prison and fed the bread of affliction and the water of affliction until Ahab returned again in peace. Micaiah told him, "If thou certainly return in peace, then hath not the Lord spoken by me" (2 Chronicles 18:27).

So the two kings prepared for battle. Ahab must have been a little nervous, because he decided to disguise himself and told Jehoshaphat to wear the robes of a king. Meanwhile, the Syrians wanted only to destroy Ahab, the king of Israel, so when their captains saw Jehoshaphat dressed in robes, they surrounded him, thinking he was the king of Israel. "But Jehoshaphat cried out, and the Lord helped him; and God moved them to depart from him" (2 Chronicles 18:31). As the day went on, Ahab was wounded, and about the time the sun went down, he died.

When Jehoshaphat returned home, he spoke to one of his own prophets whom he could trust. The prophet told him, "Shouldest thou help the ungodly, and love them that hate the Lord? therefore is wrath upon thee from before the Lord. Nevertheless there are good things found in thee, in that thou . . . hast prepared thine heart to seek God" (2 Chronicles 19:2–3).

We are taught an important lesson from this account: Jehoshaphat had entered into a great undertaking without the sanction of the Lord. Since he had already entered into an alliance with a wicked man, it became troublesome to inquire of the Lord, for regardless of what the prophet said, it was now too late to withdraw. "In truth, it was only what may always be expected when those who serve and love the Lord allow themselves to be entangled in alliances with ungodly men, where one step leads to another, and one inconsistency involves the next, till at last we recoil when it is too late to withdraw, and the only thing consistent is to be inconsistent in owning God where His will can no longer be obeyed. But even this is good, for it is the first step to repentance. And though we must suffer the punishment of our folly, yet God will hear a Jehoshaphat in the disastrous battle, when he crieth to Him, *and give gracious deliverance*" (Alfred Edersheim, *Bible History,* 6:62, emphasis added).

When was the last time you received prophetic counsel? How could you apply the truths you heard?

Sometimes our choices are going to be wrong. Like Jehoshaphat, we might find ourselves in a situation we can't get out of on our own. Our first thought might be that we don't qualify for the grace He extends to us, or perhaps we feel strong enough to walk the road alone.

The Lord allows us to have choices. He will not force us to turn to Him. However, a day may come when we cry out for help. The Lord's response is certain every time. He will hear a Jehoshaphat. He knows the good to be found in us because He knows each of our hearts. In the disastrous battle, when we cry out to Him, He will be there. From Jehoshaphat we learn the importance of listening to the words of the prophet. Often the counsel from God's prophet here on earth can prevent us from even entering a battle we do not wish to participate in. "Believe in the Lord your God, so shall ye be established; believe his prophets, so shall ye prosper" (2 Chronicles 20:20).

The Battle Is Not Yours

During the reign of King Jehoshaphat, a great multitude came against him from beyond the sea. In this moment of great need, he did what he had always done: "he set himself to seek the Lord" (2 Chronicles 20:3).

During this preparation time before the battle, the king proclaimed a fast throughout all the land, and then he stood in front of the house of the Lord and prayed, remembering a covenant the Lord had made with them: "If, when evil cometh upon us, as the sword, judgment, or pestilence, or famine, we stand before this house, and in thy presence, (for thy name is in this house,) and cry unto thee in our affliction, then thou wilt hear and help. . . . O our God, . . . we have no might against this great company that cometh against us; *neither know we what to do: but our eyes are upon thee*" (2 Chronicles 20:9, 12; emphasis added).

How many times in our own lives have each of us brought that challenge to the Lord? *I don't know what to do.* In these moments, when what is against us seems mightier than we are, how often is our first inclination to focus our eyes upon the Lord? To set ourselves to seek Him? How often do we look to our own strength first? Maybe we are good at problem solving. Too many times our first course of action is a practical one rather than a spiritual one. Perhaps in moments like these we can look to Jehoshaphat—a man who set himself to seek God first, always.

So King Jehoshaphat petitioned the Lord in all of Israel's behalf. "And all Judah stood before the Lord, with their little ones, their wives, and their children. Then . . . came the Spirit of the Lord in the midst of the congregation; And he said, Hearken ye, all Judah, and ye inhabitants of Jerusalem, and thou king Jehoshaphat, Thus saith the Lord unto you, Be not afraid nor dismayed by reason of this great multitude*; for the battle is not yours, but God's*" (2 Chronicles 20:13–15; emphasis added).

Think of the greatest trial you face right now; consider your multitude of burdens. Have you set yourself to seek God?

Think of the greatest trial you face right now; consider your multitude of burdens. Have you set yourself to seek God? In the hour of greatest indecision, are you prepared to look to the Lord? Our God is great.

He is mightier than any multitude of burdens we could ever face. Only He can fight our battles, because only He knows what it will take to conquer them. When we set ourselves to seek Him, we will be able to heed the final counsel the Lord gave to King Jehoshaphat, "To morrow go out against them: for the Lord will be with you" (2 Chronicles 20:17). As we learn to recognize that the Lord is with us in every battle, we are able to discern the Spirit of the Lord as it descends upon us and to focus on His calming words, "the battle is not yours, but God's."

Sometimes, as we face our greatest challenges, all that is required is to stand before His house, in His presence, and cry unto Him. In such times we must believe that He will hear and help. We must trust that He will be with us. This battle is not ours, but His. President Ezra Taft Benson counseled the Saints who would live in the last days: "The final outcome is certain—the forces of righteousness will win. What remains to be seen is *where* each of us personally, now and in the future, will stand in this fight—and *how tall* we will stand. . . . [Jesus Christ] is the most successful warrior that ever walked the earth, and He wants to help us win every battle" ("In His Steps," 2; emphasis in original).

When our trials seem to overtake us, in the moments when we find ourselves overwhelmed by the multitude of our burdens, perhaps it would help if we were to remember Jehoshaphat's example. We must never forget: the battle is not ours, but God's—and He is with us.

Heaps of Blessings

The first thing Hezekiah did when he began to reign was to open the doors of the temple. There is significance in this event, for it was in his heart "to make a covenant with the Lord God of Israel" (2 Chronicles 29:10). But Hezekiah was not satisfied with just making a change in his own life. His capacity to love and to lead was magnified, and he extended the invitation to "all Israel and Judah, and wrote letters also to Ephraim and Manasseh, that they should come to the house of the Lord at Jerusalem" (2 Chronicles 30:1). Some laughed him to scorn and mocked him, but some humbled themselves and came. "And they stood in their place" (2 Chronicles 30:16). From a simple invitation extended by a humble man, a very great congregation gathered. "And Hezekiah rejoiced, and all the people, that God had prepared the people: *for the thing was done suddenly*" (2 Chronicles 29:36; emphasis added).

This story reminds me of the great power that one righteous person can have. It testifies to the power of one in changing the lives of many. I love that it can happen suddenly. What can we learn about leadership from the story of Hezekiah? The scriptures tell us he had a gift for speaking to the heart. Encouragingly. Intimately.

He prayed for his people, asking the Lord to pardon everyone and to heal them. He "wrought that which was good and right and truth before the Lord his God" (2 Chronicles 31:20). But my favorite characteristic of all is found in this verse: "In every work that he began . . . he did it with all his heart" (2 Chronicles 31:21).

Because of these characteristics, the people gathered to him. "And the people rested themselves [or relied] upon the words of Hezekiah king of Judah" (2 Chronicles 32:8). The Lord fought their battles, guided them on every side, and blessed them. Through Hezekiah's leadership, the people learned to be encouraged in the laws of the Lord. This allowed great blessings to come to them.

One way the blessings were manifest was through the heaps or the storehouses for the tithes. One day Hezekiah came to see the heaps. Azariah, the chief priest, told Hezekiah, "Since the people began to bring the offerings into the house of the Lord, we have had enough to eat, and have left plenty: for the Lord hath blessed his people; and that which is left is this great store" (2 Chronicles 31:10). I love the image of these heaps, these storehouses, filled with the blessings poured out from the Lord, a blessing so big there was not room enough to receive it—heaps of blessings.

> "Since the people began to bring the offerings . . . the Lord hath blessed his people." When have you experienced a blessing from paying tithing?

When I read this story, I am reminded of a scripture found in Malachi, "Bring ye all the tithes into the storehouse . . . and prove me now herewith, saith the Lord of hosts, if I will not open you the *windows of heaven,* and pour you out a blessing, that there shall not be room enough to receive it" (Malachi 3:10; emphasis added). Here in 2 Chronicles is another witness of the promise penned in Malachi—a blessing so great that there shall not be room enough to receive it. The lesson of Hezekiah is clear: heaps of blessings will come, and it can happen suddenly.

Stand to It

During the reign of Josiah, a sacred book was found in the house of the Lord. Josiah asked those who had the book, "Go, enquire of the Lord for me . . . concerning the words of the book" (2 Chronicles 34:21).

Then Josiah, the king whose heart was tender, sent and gathered together all the elders, and "the men of Judah, and the inhabitants of Jerusalem, and the priests, and the Levites, and all the people, *great and small:* and he read in their ears all the words of the book of the covenant that was found in the house of the Lord.

"And the king *stood in his place,* and made a covenant before the Lord, to walk after the Lord, and to keep his commandments, and his testimonies, and his statutes, with all his heart, and with all his soul, to perform the words of the covenant which are written in this book. And he caused all that were present in Jerusalem . . . to *stand to it.* And the inhabitants of Jerusalem did" (2 Chronicles 34:30–32; emphasis added).

Josiah didn't just gather his people together, he read in their ears all the words of the book of the covenant. I see a lesson here—just the gathering is not enough. In our family we gather together to eat, and to play, and to snuggle, and to be entertained, but in this world just the gathering together is insufficient. When we gather together, we must read the words of the Book. Therein lies the strength.

We must learn to keep the commandments and the testimonies and the statutes with all our heart and with all our soul, and then *stand to it* and act upon what we learn.

When our home was being built, my family would stop by every evening to watch the progress. One evening we came just after the footings had been laid but before the cement floor had been poured. We talked about foundations as we stood there in a circle, every one of us—*the great and the small.* We told our children that if the foundation was firm, it would provide a base for something to stand on—our home. It is the same with a testimony. If our testimony is firm, it creates a solid base for us to stand on. We wanted to remember that a firm foundation would allow us to stand for what we believed in, so we talked about what would make our foundation firm. We came up with an acronym: **S**criptures **T**estimony **A**nd Prayer **N**ight and **D**ay—**STAND**. Then we each took off one of our shoes, and we buried the shoes in the ground next to one of the footings. The next day they poured cement over the hole. The shoes remain buried inside our foundation today as a reminder of the testimony of the covenant we made—to stand.

What is one way you could "stand to it" today?

One of the few hymns that is written from the perspective of the Lord speaking to His children is also one of my very favorite hymns. In it, the Lord tells us:

> *Fear not, I am with thee; oh, be not dismayed,*
> *For I am thy God and will still give thee aid.*
> I'll strengthen thee, help thee, and cause thee to stand,
> *Upheld by my righteous, omnipotent hand.*
> ("How Firm a Foundation," *Hymns,* no. 85; emphasis added)

I Am Doing a Great Work

Nehemiah's humble prayer touched my heart. He prayed for the walls of Jerusalem to be repaired and the gates to be mended. The burden consumed his countenance. When the king asked why he was sad, Nehemiah replied, "Why should not my countenance be sad, when the city, the place of my fathers' sepulchers, lieth waste, and the gates thereof are consumed with fire?" The king asked him, "For what dost thou make request?" Nehemiah's answer consisted of five simple words, "that I may build it" (Nehemiah 2:3–5). He arose in the night and viewed the wall surrounding Jerusalem. He saw the destruction and understood the work that would be required. Then he gathered the people together, saying, "See the distress that we are in . . . come, and let us build up the wall of Jerusalem" (Nehemiah 2:17).

The people came together and prepared to work. Meanwhile, the enemies of Jerusalem also gathered. They pointed fingers at the people, despising them, and as they laughed they said, "What is this thing that ye do?" Nehemiah answered, "The God of heaven, he will prosper us; therefore we his servants will arise and build" (Nehemiah 2:19–20). As they worked, the enemy wondered about the people who were building, and he asked his men, "Will they fortify themselves? will they sacrifice?" (Nehemiah 4:2). These wicked men conspired against the people who were building, day and night.

So Nehemiah gathered the people together again. He armed them with swords and spears and bows, and he told them: "Be not ye afraid of them: remember the Lord. . . . The work is great and large, and we are separated upon the wall, one far from another. In what place therefore ye hear the sound of the trumpet . . . resort ye thither unto us: our God shall fight for us" (Nehemiah 4:14, 19–20). So they returned to the wall, "every one unto his work" (Nehemiah 4:15).

They began to build again, but this time was different. Now the people built with one hand and carried a weapon with them at all times in the other hand. "For the people had a mind to work" (Nehemiah 4:6).

When the enemy found out that the people continued to work, they wanted to speak to Nehemiah. They asked him to come down from what he was doing and meet with them. And he replied, "I am doing a great work, so that I cannot come down: why should the work cease, whilst I leave it and come down to you?" (Nehemiah 6:3).

Four times the enemy asked Nehemiah to come down, and every time he answered them the same, "I am doing a great work, so that I cannot come down." Finally, the fifth time they sent Nehemiah a letter saying, "Come now therefore, and let us take counsel together" (Nehemiah 6:7). They tried to make Nehemiah afraid. But he would not come down, and finally he replied, "Should such a man as I flee?" (Nehemiah 6:11).

"What a remarkable response! With that clear and unchanging purpose of heart and mind, with that great resolve, the walls of Jerusalem rose until they were rebuilt in an astonishing fifty-two days.

"Nehemiah refused to allow distractions to prevent him from doing what the Lord wanted him to do. . . .

"Like Nehemiah, we have a great work to do. We stand overlooking the horizon of our age. It is my fervent prayer that in spite of temptations, we will never lower our standards; that in spite of distractions, wherever they may come from, we will not lose focus on what matters most; that we will stand resolute and together, shoulder to shoulder, as we valiantly bear the banner of the Lord Jesus Christ" (Dieter F. Uchtdorf, "We Are Doing a Great Work," 61–62).

What is the greatest work in your life right now? Have you sought the Lord in fasting and prayer? What is your request?

Consider your greatest work right now. What is it? Have you gone to the Lord in prayer? In fasting? Make your request, and then get to work. Build. Others may question your resolve to fortify your efforts, to sacrifice. Be not afraid of them. Remember the Lord. You are doing a great work—do not come down!

Thanks Giving

In the book of Nehemiah we read of a priest named Mattaniah, "which was over the thanksgiving" (Nehemiah 12:8). I am fascinated by him, and I have decided for my next job I want to be the person over the thanks giving.

Imagine what would fill your thoughts if you were constantly in charge of giving thanks.

What if it were your job "to praise and to give thanks" all day, every single day? (Nehemiah 12:24).

On the day the walls of Jerusalem were dedicated, two great companies were sent up upon the wall to give thanks, "Then I brought up the princes of Judah upon the wall, and appointed two great companies of them that gave thanks" (Nehemiah 12:31).

I can picture Ezra leading one company with musical instruments down the one side of the wall, a second company with musical instruments walking down the other side of the wall with Nehemiah following behind, and certain of the priests' sons following with trumpets. The companies had been appointed for one reason—to give thanks.

I would have loved to have been there on that day to witness the thanksgiving, the rejoicing, the great joy—so great that it was heard even afar off. "Also that day they offered great sacrifices, and rejoiced: for God had made them rejoice with great joy: the wives also and the children rejoiced: so that the joy of Jerusalem was heard even afar off" (Nehemiah 12:43). Did you notice that it was God who had made them rejoice with great joy?

Consider putting yourself in charge of the thanks giving for today. How might you rejoice with great joy?

I wonder if today could be a day like that, filled with rejoicing and great joy and thanks giving. I think it could. What if we decided to put ourselves in charge of the thanks giving today? Starting from sunup, we could fill our thoughts with gratitude, rejoicing, and giving thanks. I want to start my morning with a prayer and ask the Lord to make me rejoice with great joy, like Nehemiah did, for the whole day, with every thought. Thanks giving.

I wonder, how full will my heart be with the setting of the sun?

How full of gratitude—how full of joy.

"O Thou who has given us so much, mercifully grant us one thing more—a grateful heart" (George Herbert).

once upon a Time

Esther's story has always been one of my favorites because it reminds me so much of a fairy tale.

Once upon a time there was a Jewish orphan named Esther. She was raised by her uncle, Mordecai. She became his daughter, and he loved her very much. One day a proclamation went forth throughout the land asking all the fair young maidens to gather to a palace where they would be trained to meet the king and be considered to become his wife. Every maiden who wanted to be considered had to pass through months of preparation, so Esther left Mordecai and went to the palace where she would be taught to meet the king.

In the kingdom there were many rules. One of the rules was that no one could talk to the king unless he called for that person by name. The penalty for talking to the king without being called for was death, so each of the maidens waited in the palace until her name was called. Now, when it was Esther's turn, she went up unto the king. The king loved Esther above all women, and so he set the crown upon her head and made her the queen. There was a great feast, and it was called Esther's feast. The king gave gifts to everyone because he was so happy.

One day a terrible thing happened. The king's adviser, Haman, who was an evil man, told all of the people they had to bow before him. Mordecai, Esther's uncle, was loyal to the king, but he refused to bow before this evil man. This made the king's adviser furious. He wanted to punish Mordecai, who was a Jew. On top of that, he wanted to punish all the Jews in the land.

The king did not know Esther was a Jew. He didn't know very much about the Jewish people. Because he trusted his adviser, he listened to what he said. Haman, the evil man, talked the king into sending out a decree that all of the Jews in the land should be killed. Queen Esther was afraid for Mordecai and all of her people. She didn't know what to do, so she sent one of her servants to ask Mordecai's advice. Mordecai told Queen Esther to go to the king and tell him that she was a Jew and ask him to save her people, who had done nothing wrong to the king.

But Esther was scared. Remember the rule of the kingdom? No one could go in to speak to the king unless they were called for by name, and Esther had not been called in to see the king. She reminded Mordecai of the grave danger she was in if she chose to approach the king. Now, here comes my favorite part of the story.

Mordecai knew how dangerous it would be for Esther to stand up for her people. He had raised Esther as his daughter, and he loved her. I imagine he must have been so worried about Esther. But still, he gave her great counsel. He reaffirmed the importance of her mission to save her people and then said, "Who knoweth whether thou art come to the kingdom for such a time as this?" (Esther 4:14). In other words, "You have been sent here to earth with a specific mission to fulfill, and the events of your life have been orchestrated such that you are in the right place at the right time, and this is your moment to shine." Now, that may have been true, but it didn't make it less scary.

Queen Esther thought long and hard about what she was about to do. Finally, she sent her servant back to Mordecai with her answer, "Go, gather together all the Jews . . . and fast ye for me, and neither eat nor drink three days, night or day: I also and my maidens will fast likewise;

and so will I go in unto the king, which is not according to the law: and if I perish, I perish" (Esther 4:16). Queen Esther decided to stand up for what she believed. In this moment, it is important to notice one essential detail—she did not go in to the king alone. Mordecai and all of the Jews were fasting for her. And she and all of her best friends were fasting. Queen Esther approached the king knowing that the strength of her people, her friends, and, most important, the Lord, was with her.

So, on the third day, even though the king had not called her name, Esther put on her fancy, royal clothing and stood in the inner court of the king's house, where the king sat upon his royal throne. When the king saw Esther, the queen, standing all dressed up in the middle of the court, he remembered how much he loved her, and he raised his golden scepter and said, "What wilt thou, queen Esther? and what is thy request?" (Esther 5:3). Queen Esther asked the king to come to a banquet, and when he did, she reminded him of the evil decree and told him she was a Jew, and then she begged him to save her life and the lives of her people. The king wondered how such an awful thing could happen, and Esther told the king that his servant was a wicked man, and his enemy. So Haman, the evil man, was put to death. And Esther and her people were saved.

> Have you ever considered why you have come to the kingdom for such a time as this?

After everything had finally calmed down, the Jews throughout the land gathered to rejoice in their deliverance and victory.

I love the description of this event found in Esther 9:19. It was described as "a day of gladness . . . and a good day."

Filling the Empty Places

I am going to be honest.

Job scares me.

I should probably clarify that I am not necessarily scared of Job, the man; I am scared of Job, the book. Reading his story brings out the realist in me and reminds me how fragile life can be. But experience has taught me that there is great wisdom found in each of the stories that have been included in the scriptures, and Job's story is no exception.

Do you know what it is to feel empty? Have you ever faced one of those moments when you have nothing left to give? Have the circumstances of life ever taken so much from you that it feels as if your whole soul has been carved out? In those moments, doesn't it seem that all that remains is a fragile vessel left empty? Who fills the empty places?

It was in the still moments of Job's life that the answer to this question became clear. "Hearken unto this, O Job; stand still, and consider the wondrous works of God" (Job 37:14). We must remember, God knew from the very beginning what was about to happen to Job. He knew about the trials, but He also knew about the blessings. More important, He knew about the learning, and what it would take to make Job's life experience complete, full—He knew how to fill the empty places in Job's soul.

"I know that thou canst do every thing . . . things too wonderful for me, which I knew not" (Job 42:2–3). Although his life was filled with disappointment and discouragement, Job was blessed abundantly. At the end of his life, every empty place was filled: "The Lord gave Job twice as much as he had before. . . . So the Lord blessed the latter end of Job more than his beginning" (Job 42:10–12). Elder Joseph B. Wirthlin explained: "The Lord compensates the faithful for every loss. That which is taken away from those who love the Lord will be added unto them in His own way. While it may not come at the time we desire, the faithful will know that every tear today will eventually be returned a hundredfold with tears of rejoicing and gratitude" ("Come What May, and Love It," 28). The Lord knows how to fill the empty places. We may not understand how, but it will be done—in the Lord's way, and in the Lord's time.

> The Lord has blessings in store, wonderful things, of which we know not. Stand still and consider some of those wondrous works today.

As much as we wish it weren't so, sometimes great moments of trial are what it takes to fill the empty places.

In the darkest moments we must remember the testimony of Job: "I know that thou canst do every thing . . . things too wonderful for me, which I knew not" (Job 42:2–3). When our soul feels empty, we must hold on to that truth. The Lord has in store things too wonderful, which we know not. Then we must stand still, and consider the wondrous works of God. If we never let go of our faith in God and put our trust and hope in Him, He will fill the fragile vessel left empty with a fulness that runneth over.

"We are the clay, and thou our potter; and we are all the work of thy hand."

Isaiah 64:8

Invitations from

The Book of Psalms, The Book of Proverbs, Ecclesiastes or, The Preacher, and The Book of the Prophet Isaiah

Look Up

One morning, as I directed my prayer to the Lord, I remembered the last two words I had read the night before, "In the morning will I direct my prayer unto thee, *and will look up*" (Psalm 5:3; emphasis added).

What does that mean, to look up? I wondered about it as I raced up the stairs to quickly edit my daughter Meg's paper before her ride came. I pondered it again as I drove my daughter Grace to school in the early dawn hours before the sun came over the mountain. It was on my mind as I went for a walk around my neighborhood. Still there as I rotated the laundry, folded warm clothes, and hung things in the closet.

What is that verse trying to teach? I pondered as I read through the letters from two missionary sons, wrote grocery lists for two different stores, and then grabbed my phone, my keys, and my list of things to do. It was as I was driving home from the grocery store that the prompting finally came: *Why don't you try it? Look up.*

I really wanted to learn the lesson, so I pulled the car over. I stopped looking at the road ahead of me, the list down in my lap, the phone sitting next to me. I opened the car door, stepped out, and looked up. The first thing I noticed was a church steeple rising into the blue sky. "But as for me, I will come into thy house in the multitude of thy mercy" (Psalm 5:7). I considered the *multitude* of His mercy, the blessings that I have experienced in that house. Many times. Too many times to count. How many times have I disregarded the multitude of His mercy?

To the left of the steeple I saw the flag blowing gently with the breeze. "But let all those that put their trust in thee rejoice: let them ever shout for joy, because thou defendest them" (Psalm 5:11). I wondered, *Do I rejoice in the knowledge that He defends me?* I have experienced His deliverance. Many times. Too many to count. But when was the last time I shouted for joy?

I turned to get back in my car and looked up one last time, noticing the canopy of pink blossoms above where I had parked my car. "Let them also that love thy name be joyful in thee" (Psalm 5:11). I love His name, but do I see it in everything around me? His signature is upon every beautiful thing, the touch of His hand everywhere. I realized that I might have neglected to see it there. Many times. Too many to count. I have missed out on His joy.

Try this: "In the morning will I direct my prayer unto thee, and will look up" (Psalm 5:3). Write down what you discover.

In that instant, my focus changed. I realized that I spend far too much time looking ahead, looking down, looking aimlessly. It is not often that I find myself looking up. My good friend Kris Belcher gives wise counsel in this regard: "We must live vertically." I love the thought of that. To live vertically will require us to look up, to become heaven focused—*to look to God.* These looking-up moments are the moments that will lead us to "stand in awe" (Psalm 4:4).

I need more moments like that.

That My Footsteps Slip Not

One weekend we went for a hike that was somewhat out of the ordinary. We walked up a riverbed, under trees and over rocks, with cool water spilling over our sandaled feet. It was one of those rare hikes you wish would just keep going. But it wasn't long before we rounded a bend and realized we could go no farther. Smooth walls climbed up both sides of the trail, and the river's path was suddenly blocked by a fifteen-foot waterfall. It was a beautiful scene, but completely impassable.

For just a moment we thought we had reached the end of the hike. Our eyes wandered longingly to the scenery that beckoned to us from up above. And then, just there to the right, we saw the footsteps that had been carefully chiseled into the rock wall.

Even now, just thinking about it, I can feel my heart sink right into my feet. There was a rope that had been anchored into the wall above, but there was also a steep drop-off below. You could see the place where the chiseled footsteps ended, but you couldn't see the even path, the sure ground, the safety waiting there. It caused reason for pause. How could you be sure that the rope would hold, the footsteps would lead to safety, the heart would not fail? Courage would be required, trust in the carver of each foothold, and faith that what lay above was worth the climb.

For some the courage came easily—they grabbed the rope, reached the destination, and called out encouragement to those waiting below.

Others found it easier with the companionship of one who had gone before, one who would walk with them and ensure that their feet would not slip. But for some the pathway was too daunting. Watching them led me to understand that no less faith is required, no less courage, no less trust, for those who are carried. It takes great courage to allow someone to lift you off your feet and carry you over the place you cannot go, to trust in the strength of the one who lifts, and to have faith that he will not fail you.

As I watched each of my family members navigate the trail, my mind filled with moments when I have faced obstacles in my way and felt my heart sinking into my toes. There have been days when I could not see the even path, the sure ground, the safety waiting there. Those are the times when courage is required—trust in the Carver of the foothold and faith that what lies ahead will be worth the climb.

Think of a daunting period in your life. Did following His path allow your footsteps to slip not?

Those moments have led me to know the Lord. "The Lord is my rock, and my fortress, and my deliverer; my God, my strength, in whom I will trust" (Psalm 18:2). I have experienced daunting moments that have required great courage—the kind of courage that allows the Deliverer to lift you off your feet and carry you over the place you cannot go. I have learned to trust in the strength of the One who lifts, to have faith that He will not fail.

Sometimes, in those most daunting moments, I breathe a silent prayer, "Hold up my goings in thy paths, that my footsteps slip not" (Psalm 17:5).

Hold me up, Lord.

In that moment there is courage, and trust, and faith.

soft with showers

For two days I had watched the gray clouds gather, felt the north wind blow, and breathed in the spring cleaning that was taking place outside my windows. But more important, I had been keeping a careful eye on the raspberries my daughters and I had transplanted just before the rain began. The weather had been just exactly right for raspberry transplants: the clouds that offered cover from the sweltering sun, the soft rain, and the heaven-sent watering. It settled the furrows, made soft the soil, and allowed for growth to begin.

My constant prayer over those raspberry shoots since the afternoon my daughters and I transplanted them has been that the conditions would be exactly what they needed to take root so they would be able to grow and thrive. I am looking forward to the sweet red berries that will soon spring from the stems growing there.

"Thou visitest the earth, and waterest it: . . . thou waterest the ridges thereof abundantly: thou settlest the furrows thereof: thou makest it soft with showers: thou blessest the springing thereof" (Psalm 65:9–10).

As I read that verse my prayer changed from raspberries to daughters, from bare roots to gospel roots. "But if ye neglect the tree, and take no thought for its nourishment, behold it will not get any root; and when the heat of the sun cometh and scorcheth it, because it hath no root it withers away, and ye pluck it up and cast it out. Now, this is not because the seed was not good, neither is it because the fruit thereof would not be desirable; but it is because your ground is barren, and ye will not nourish the tree, therefore ye cannot have the fruit thereof" (Alma 32:38–39).

What inspiration have you received lately that might help your children to take root, grow, and thrive?

Again I find myself looking to the heavens. Might He send rain in the form of inspiration to water my daughters' souls abundantly, to settle the furrows, and to make their hearts soft? As I see the young and tender roots there, this is the prayer of my mother heart—may the Lord bless the springing thereof.

In speaking to the young women of the Church, President Thomas S. Monson said: "Unless the roots of your testimony are firmly planted, it will be difficult for you to withstand the ridicule of those who challenge your faith. When firmly planted, your testimony of the gospel, of the Savior, and of Heavenly Father will influence all that you do throughout your life. . . . Your testimony, when constantly nourished, will keep you safe" ("May You Have Courage," 126).

To Bear Thee Up

Have you ever had one of those moments when you are not sure if you can put one foot in front of the other?

Maybe the trail has been going uphill for longer than you anticipated. Or perhaps the load you carry is too heavy for one person to bear alone. Sometimes you feel it when you turn a corner only to realize the end is nowhere in sight. Your thoughts fill with doubt and discouragement. You wonder how you arrived at this course, this journey, this destination, because you're pretty sure you might not make it through to the end.

In fact, you're not quite sure you can even take one more step.

How do we make it through those moments?

"For he shall give his angels charge over thee, to keep thee in all thy ways. They shall bear thee up in their hands, lest thou dash thy foot against a stone" (Psalm 91:11–12).

I believe angels are real. In the moments of discouragement and doubt when I haven't the strength to put one foot in front of the other, the Lord has sent angels to bear me up, to strengthen me, and to help lift the heavy load. Because of them I have made it through things I could never have made it through on my own.

"I have spoken . . . of heavenly help, of angels dispatched to bless us in time of need. But when we speak of those who are instruments in the hand of God, we are reminded that not all angels are from the other side of the veil. Some of them we walk with and talk with—here, now, every day. Some of them reside in our own neighborhoods" (Jeffrey R. Holland, "The Ministry of Angels," 30). Some of them reside in our own homes.

I don't know what your circumstances are today. Perhaps you are in desperate need of heaven's help. If so, I pray the Lord will give His angels charge over you. But even more important, I pray that He will open your eyes to recognize the angels that He sends. We must remember that angels come in different shapes and sizes, and bearing up comes in ways we might not anticipate.

Think about who you could help. Would you be willing in the next week to act upon your promptings?

If your circumstances right now do not require bearing up, if all is well in your life, maybe you could set aside time this week to be on the errand of angels, to share your gift, to do whatsoever is gentle, to cheer and to bless (see "As Sisters in Zion," *Hymns,* no. 309).

Great peace comes from the knowledge that His angels have charge over each one of us. No matter what your circumstances are or where your steps may lead, may His angels keep thee, watch over thee, and bear thee up.

Today, and always.

These Seven Things

In Proverbs 6 is a list of things the Lord hates, "These six things doth the Lord hate: yea, seven are an abomination unto him" (Proverbs 6:16). I was a little nervous to read past that verse. I just *knew* there would be things on the list I struggled with. Sure enough, there were. Reading through the list gave me a gentle reminder of some areas in my life that might need a little work. Here are the seven things the Lord doth hate:

1. A proud look
2. A lying tongue
3. Hands that shed innocent blood
4. An heart that deviseth wicked imaginations
5. Feet that be swift in running to mischief
6. A false witness that speaketh lies (including slander or gossip)
7. He that soweth discord among brethren (Proverbs 6:17–19)

Immediately I noticed that I needed to keep a close watch on my eyes, my tongue, my hands, my heart, and my feet. But it was the last two that really stood out to me. It never occurred to me that one could be called a false witness for spreading gossip, rumors, or slander—but I agree with that designation. I don't ever want to be found in that category, even by mistake. So I am going to become more careful in that area than I already try to be.

My mind has also been caught up with what it means to sow

discord. When we were little, my dad would always counsel us not to "stir the pot." That is the first phrase that came to mind when I read the words *soweth discord.* A good definition for *discord* is lack of harmony. Sometimes in my spare time I play the piano, and a difficult song may lead to my fingers landing on the wrong notes within a chord. Just that one wrong chord can ruin the entire piece.

That is how powerful discord is. Rather than creating unity, sowing discord can be extremely divisive. It has the power to destroy peace. I don't want to do that, so in order to avoid it, I must learn the opposite of sowing discord. In my mind that would be one who spreads harmony, peace, or unity. That is who I want to be.

If the opposite of something the Lord hates would be a quality the Lord loves, what would happen if we could learn to live the opposite qualities of all the things the Lord doth hate? Would each of those attributes become things the Lord doth love?

1. A humble view
2. A truthful speech
3. Hands that protect and nurture
4. A heart that deviseth wise thoughts
5. Feet that are swift in running to good
6. A true witness that speaketh compliments
7. He that spreads harmony among brethren

Which one of the seven good attributes would you most like to acquire?

These are seven areas I would like to work on, but I am coming to understand that just having the desire isn't enough—I must commit to live these opposites of the seven things. I may not be able to achieve this all at once, but one at a time, I can learn to overcome the things the Lord doth hate.

A Brother Born for Adversity

It was the year Josh was in fourth grade and Caleb was in sixth. I was in my bathroom getting ready for the day. I could hear the boys getting ready for school upstairs. Then the banging began—loud banging, and yelling. *What could they be arguing about at this time of day?* I wondered as I left the serenity of my room for the catastrophe upstairs.

It was as I arrived at the bottom of the stairs that I realized it wasn't an argument; it was an emergency. The one we had planned for, but prayed would never happen. I could hear it in Caleb's voice as he cried out my name over and over, "Mom! Mom! Mom!" Josh, in a diabetic hypoglycemic state of unawareness, had climbed into the bathtub where Caleb was bathing, slipped under the water, and started to have a seizure. Caleb, the older brother caught unaware, had done the smartest thing. He reached his arms under Josh's, lifted his head and shoulders out of the water, and began calling my name. I will never forget his tiny frame being knocked violently against the water spout as he held Josh above the water with all his might until I came running frantically up the stairs and pulled him out of the tub onto the bathroom floor. I won't forget the red marks already bruising along his spine. I won't forget twelve-year-old Caleb on the phone with 911 trying to direct the ambulance to our home while I gave Josh a shot filled with sugar, made sure he continued to breathe, and held him so he wouldn't hurt himself.

I won't forget Caleb, standing silently over his brother as the paramedics came, watching. He wouldn't leave for school until he knew his brother was safe, until he knew everything was going to be okay.

That was the memory that filled my mind when I read this verse: "A friend loveth at all times, and a brother is born for adversity" (Proverbs 17:17).

Could you be the kind of friend who lifts another who is drowning, protects someone from pain, provides watchcare, companionship, and loyalty? What does it mean to you to love at all times?

Wouldn't it be a blessing if we could all learn to be that kind of friend? The kind of friend who lifts another who is drowning. Who protects them from pain. Who seeks the help that will bring healing. Who provides watchcare, companionship, and loyalty. A friend who loveth at all times, even on the very worst days, through the moments you prayed would never happen, when the serenity of life turns to catastrophe. The kind of friend Mason Canon described, "The person we all love and appreciate is the one who's coming in the door when everybody else is going out."

Perhaps today each of us could try to be a friend like that.

"Two are better than one . . . for if they fall, the one will lift up his fellow" (Ecclesiastes 4:9–10).

Five Reasons to Love the Book of Isaiah

There are not enough words to describe my great love of Isaiah, but I hope that somehow these thoughts will make it from the innermost place in my heart and find a place in yours. Perhaps you grew up in the same generation that I did—the one where everyone told you to skip the Isaiah chapters when you read the Book of Mormon. When you wondered why, those same people told you that you wouldn't be able to understand them. Perhaps you believed them. If that has been your experience, then I am going to ask you to set that all aside, because lots of times people think they don't like peas, or avocados, or crème brûlée. Then they try the thing they thought they hated, only to find out they actually like it—a lot. Gratitude comes in that moment for the simple fact that they won't go through the rest of their lives missing out on something they didn't know they were going to love so much. In case that might happen for you, I am going to share with you five reasons why I love Isaiah.

1. "That I might more fully persuade them to believe in the Lord their Redeemer I did read unto them that which was written by the prophet Isaiah" (1 Nephi 19:23). Isaiah has a beautiful way of expressing his belief in the Savior. It is poetic and visual, and he teaches us characteristics of the Lord in a way that is different from any other book of

scripture. As you read Isaiah this time, watch for verses that testify of Christ. Mark them. Learn from them.

2. "Surely he spake as touching all things" (3 Nephi 23:2). Within the pages of Isaiah you will find his testimony on many gospel principles, including tithing, fast offerings, the Atonement, the Church in the latter days, the stakes of Zion, and the temple, among others. This time when you read Isaiah, watch for verses that speak counsel and also verses that speak warning. What can you learn from them?

> What is your favorite verse from the great words in the book of Isaiah?

3. "In the days that the prophecies of Isaiah shall be fulfilled men shall know of a surety, at the times when they shall come to pass" (2 Nephi 25:7). The book of Isaiah contains many prophecies, some of which have already come to pass and others that are still to come. As you read Isaiah, watch for prophecies—both those that have been fulfilled and those that will be.

4. "They shall be of great worth unto them in the last days; for in that day shall they understand them; wherefore, for their good have I written them" (2 Nephi 25:8). Nephi has given us a great promise. We live in the last days, which means we are the people who will understand the words of Isaiah. What an incredible gift! This time as you read Isaiah, pray for the Spirit to be with you, then have faith in the promise given by Nephi: you *will* understand his words.

5. "Search these things diligently; for great are the words of Isaiah" (3 Nephi 23:1). This is something I believe with all my heart. Take your time. Read slowly. Soak it in. As you turn each page, remind yourself of that truth: *great* are the words of Isaiah. Believe it, and it will be so.

Sometimes Life Requires Us to Shoulder a Heavy Load

When you think of the word *yoke,* you probably think of the wooden yoke with two sides used by a pair of oxen. But have you ever seen a single yoke? This type of yoke is made of sturdy leather with metal rungs, and it is used by a horse required to pull an oppressive or burdensome load. The yoke cannot be removed by the one who is harnessed in it. It has been crafted to withstand intense pressure, maximum loads, and exhausting work.

The details and the imagery of this single yoke caused me to wonder if we know the oppression of being yoked in our world today. Obviously, we are not yoked to heavy equipment meant to be dragged through fields or furrows, but consider those who are burdened by debt, by addiction, by sorrow, or by fear.

Sometimes life requires us to shoulder a heavy load. It might be one we have not chosen. Often it is one from which we cannot get free. But sometimes the burden comes from the one who entangles, the one who speaks lies, the one who is intent on destroying all that is good. His burden, his yoke, is one that holds us back, that oppresses, that leads to great sorrow.

If we are yoked to this type of burden, or if someone who is dear to us shoulders this kind of load, we must remember that all is not lost: "And it shall come to pass in that day, that *his* burden shall be taken away from off thy shoulder, and *his* yoke from off thy neck, and the yoke shall be destroyed *because of the anointing*" (Isaiah 10:27; emphasis added). The Bible Dictionary explains that "the English word *Christ* is from a Greek word meaning *anointed,* and is the equivalent of *Messiah,* which is from a Hebrew and Aramaic term meaning *anointed*" (Bible Dictionary, s.v. "Anointed One"). There *is* One who can give us rest from bondage, who can remove the yoke. He is the Anointed One. "The Spirit of the Lord God is upon me; because the Lord hath anointed me to preach good tidings unto the meek; he hath sent me to bind up the brokenhearted, to proclaim liberty to the captives, and the opening of the prison to them that are bound; . . . to comfort all that mourn; . . . to give unto them beauty for ashes, the oil of joy for mourning, the garment of praise for the spirit of heaviness" (Isaiah 61:1–3). He is Jesus Christ, the Holy One of Israel, the Anointed One. He offers rest and relief from oppression. He will make our burdens light (see Matthew 11:30).

Are you in bondage, or do you know someone who is yoked to something oppressive or burdensome? How could turning to the Anointed One set you free?

"And it shall come to pass . . . that the Lord shall give thee rest from thy sorrow, and from thy fear, and from the hard bondage wherein thou wast made to serve" (Isaiah 14:3). Are you in bondage, or is there someone close to you who is yoked to something oppressive or burdensome? Turn to the Lord, the Anointed One, Jesus Christ, the Messiah. The yoke will be destroyed *because* of the anointing.

Because of Him.

Through Him.

The potter's clay

Michelangelo's *Pietà* is a statue of Mary, the mother of Jesus, holding her son after the Crucifixion. There is something unique about this sculpture: It is the only work Michelangelo ever signed. There is a story that surrounds the signing of Michelangelo's name told by his good friend Giorgio Vasari. Shortly after the sculpture went on display, it is said that Michelangelo overheard someone remark that Michelangelo could not have sculpted it—he was too young. People said it was the work of another sculptor, Cristoforo Solari. After hearing this remark, in the late hours of the night, Michelangelo chiseled one sentence onto Mary's sash, "Michaelangelus Bonarotus Florentinus Facibat" (Michelangelo Buonarroti, Florentine, made this.) It is said that Michelangelo later regretted his pride in that moment, and vowed never to sign another work.

There is much I love about this story. I am impressed that Michelangelo was able to convey so much emotion about the Atonement in a piece of art at such a young age. Surely his testimony is captured within the beauty of the work. I love that should there be any doubt as to the validity of the testimony sculpted by his hands, he signed his name. *Michelangelo made this.* I find it remarkable that the only work Michelangelo ever signed was his testimony of the Atonement. This story reminds me that I want to be willing to sign my name to what

I know to be true even when people don't believe my testimony. *Emily Freeman believes this.* I want my life to reflect my belief.

But there is a deeper lesson we learn; it is taught in the words of Isaiah. "Surely your turning of things upside down shall be esteemed as the potter's clay: for shall the work say of him that made it, He made me not?" (Isaiah 29:16). I can't help but remember those who questioned the skill of the maker who created the *Pietà,* of Michelangelo, of his ability. Now my thoughts turn higher. I think of the Master, the Creator, the Maker, and wonder how many of us question our own worth in the hands of the Potter. Isaiah gives us a profound reminder: "Ye have not looked unto the maker thereof, neither had respect unto him that fashioned it long ago" (Isaiah 22:11). The footnote next to the word *maker* explains, "you have not turned to the Lord."

"We are the clay, and thou our potter; and we are all the work of thy hand" (Isaiah 64:8). How does knowing that make you feel?

I am reminded of the days that I question my worth, my abilities, my importance. What does the Maker think to Himself on those days? Does He wish He could reach down with His fingertip and somehow remind me, "Jesus Christ made this"? Oh, if we could only see our worth in His eyes! If only we could understand the potential He has in mind for us. If only we could visualize the beauty of His work in each one of us, individually. If only we would allow Him to shape us and mold us into who He knows we can be.

What if, on our darkest days, we remembered to look unto the Maker? How different would our perspective be?

"At that day shall a man look to his Maker, and his eyes shall have respect to the Holy One of Israel" (Isaiah 17:7).

finding the wellspring

When I was very young, my family would visit Cascade Springs, located at the top of American Fork Canyon. We walked along small rivers and past waterfalls until we reached the higher ground where we found the wellspring—a place where the water flowed out of seemingly impermeable rock before it began cascading down the mountain. It was the very spot where the spring began. Amazingly, the water never stopped; there was an overflowing fullness. In fact, each day seven million gallons of water comes through that rock base to feed the springs below.

Every time I read chapter 58 of Isaiah, I think about Cascade Springs. This chapter explains the great promises given to those who live the true law of the fast. First, I love the four reasons for fasting defined within these verses: to loose the bands of wickedness, to undo the heavy burdens, to let the oppressed go free, and to break every yoke. We are also reminded of the importance of fast offerings in relation to the law of the fast, that we must deal our bread to the hungry, remember the poor and the naked and those within our circle of influence who are struggling (see Isaiah 58:6–7).

After being given the reasons and the law, we are taught the blessings of the fast in Isaiah 58:8–10:

- Your light will "break forth as the morning, and thine health shall spring forth speedily."

• "Thy righteousness shall go before thee; the glory of the Lord shall be thy rereward" (or rearguard).

• When you call, the Lord shall answer, when you cry, the Lord shall say, Here I am.

• "Thy light [will] rise in obscurity, and thy darkness be as the noonday." (I can't help but think of answers that come in the darkest moments, and light when we need it most.)

"A spring of water, whose waters fail not . . ." Which of these blessings are you most in need of at this time?

Then we come to my favorite verse, the verse that reminds me so much of Cascade Springs, "And the Lord shall guide thee continually, and satisfy thy soul in drought, and make fat thy bones: *and thou shalt be like a watered garden, and like a spring of water, whose waters fail not*" (Isaiah 58:11; emphasis added). The footnotes for that verse speak of divine guidance, strength, and an abundant life. These are the blessings that come from living the true law of the fast. I love the thought of the Lord guiding us continually, but I especially love the image of the spring of water whose waters fail not. Just like Cascade Springs, through the fast we receive an overflowing fullness, an abundance.

Every time I read this chapter, I pause for just a moment to consider the importance of keeping the true law of the fast—the reasons, the blessings, the promises. The next time you fast, perhaps you might remember this counsel from Isaiah, open your heart to recognize the blessings, and be led to remember the Wellspring from whence those blessings flow.

"Make bright the arrows; gather the shields: . . .
Set up the standard . . . make the watch strong."

JEREMIAH 51:11–12

Invitations from

The Book of the Prophet Jeremiah, The Lamentations of Jeremiah, The Book of the Prophet Ezekiel, and The Book of Daniel

why do we sit still?

Every time I begin reading the Book of Mormon, my imagination is stirred. I can't help but wonder about the conditions of Jerusalem during Lehi's time period. I think of my own children and I wonder how bad the world around me would have to get before I would leave behind my home, my belongings, my neighbors, and my lifestyle to wander out into the wilderness and live in a tent. Don't get me wrong, I like to camp, but I also like to come home from camping. When I picture Lehi packing up his entire family and leaving his home and possessions to live in a tent, it makes me think that things in Jerusalem must have been pretty bad.

The book of Jeremiah in the Old Testament paints a picture of what life would have been like in Jerusalem during Lehi's time. Jeremiah and Lehi were contemporaries, so the Jerusalem that Lehi left is the same Jerusalem Jeremiah is writing about. As I read the words of Jeremiah, I begin to understand the hardship of raising a righteous family in an increasingly wicked world. Within the dangers his words become more clear.

Besides the gross wickedness and sin, Jeremiah defines this time period of Jerusalem with descriptions such as these: "They are not valiant for the truth . . . they know not me" (Jeremiah 9:3); "no man repented him of his wickedness" (Jeremiah 8:6); they "went backward, and not forward" (Jeremiah 7:24); this people have "a rebellious heart" (Jeremiah 5:23). He spoke of "families that call not on thy name" (Jeremiah 10:25), and how they "went after other gods to serve them" (Jeremiah 11:10). In chapter 10 Jeremiah describes the gods Israel chose to worship instead of the Lord, "for one cutteth a tree out of the forest, the work of the hands of the workman, with the axe. They deck it with silver and with gold; they fasten it with nails and with hammers, *that it move not.* They are upright as the palm tree, *but speak not:* . . . Be not afraid of them; for they cannot do evil, neither also is it in them to do good" (Jeremiah 10:3–5; emphasis added). I find myself wondering why Israel would choose to worship a god like this—one that cannot move, speak, or do good.

Do we do that today? *Obviously* we don't have a God made out of wood and decked with silver and gold . . . *or do we?* I think of our cars and our homes and our playthings and the time we devote to paying for and maintaining those items, and I pause to wonder if my adoration is fixed on items made of chrome and silver. Where is it that I am focusing most of my time? What is it that I worship most? A sport? A hobby? A possession? Oh, I hope not. I see the counsel given by Jeremiah, "*Consider ye* . . ." (Jeremiah 9:17; emphasis added).

So I consider, am I willing to be more like Lehi and let my possessions become of lesser consequence and the spirituality of my family become of greatest importance? Is there a way to live in the world, but not be of the world? Could I follow the Liahona a little bit more carefully here in my own home? Can I learn from Jeremiah what will be required for me to not walk the path Israel chose?

The prophet Jeremiah gave two warnings to his people that we can learn from today. First he asked, "Why do we sit still?" (Jeremiah 8:14). The Jerusalem Nephi grew up in was described by Jeremiah as being sensual and materialistic. Lehi decided he couldn't afford to sit still and let that environment destroy his children. I can't help but think of our world today. Do we allow wickedness to surround us through conversations, through media, through daily life, while we just sit still? Or do we assemble our family and make a plan of defense?

The second counsel Jeremiah gives is this, "To whom shall I speak, and give warning, that they may hear? . . . I am weary with holding in" (Jeremiah 6:10–11). I want to hear the warnings from our prophet today. I want to choose righteousness. I want to walk the path that will allow me to know the Lord. To really know Him. To understand Him. I don't want the prophet today to feel weary with holding in. I want to hear his words and follow them.

What is one way you could decide to not sit still today?

I want to be the type of person that Jeremiah describes, "But let him that glorieth glory in this, that he understandeth and knoweth me, that I am the Lord which exercise lovingkindness, judgment, and righteousness, in the earth: *for in these things I delight,* saith the Lord" (Jeremiah 9:24; emphasis added). Instead of choosing a god that can't move or speak, I want to choose the living God, the One who delights in lovingkindness—a God who is able to do good. So I will learn from Lehi. My possessions matter least. My family matters most. I will heed the warnings; I will choose the Lord, to worship Him.

I will not sit still.

whose Hope the Lord Is

Remember when I told you that I went on a river hike? Well, at the very beginning of the hike my nephew, Camden, said to me, "Oh, M, I have to show you my favorite tree. You're just gonna love this tree."

"What am I going to love about it?" I asked him.

"You're just gonna love it," he replied. So we hiked: him running ahead and then turning around to wait, me walking through the river, walking up the trails, climbing over rocks, watching for *the tree.* I wasn't sure how he would know we had reached the tree. We had passed hundreds of trees already and I could see more in front of us. Lining the entire riverbed were trees of all different kinds, shapes, and sizes. *What is it,* I wondered, *that sets his tree apart from the others?*

Then we came around a bend, and without him even having to say a word, I knew we had reached *the tree.* And he was right—I loved it. I am not sure why I loved it so much, but I did. Immediately. Perhaps it was the shade it provided across the entire path. It might have been the rocks that seemed strategically placed by nature itself to offer a place of rest and refuge from the heat. It could have been the boughs that stretched across the path on one side and over the river on the other. Strong boughs, just right for climbing in. Boughs that had a large curve every so often along the branch, almost as if the tree had prepared a sitting place for those who chose to venture there. It was, by far, the largest tree along the riverbank. The trunk was old and weathered. The tallest branches reached high above the other trees that lined the path. As I stood there, sheltered by its shade, I couldn't help but wonder what stories it could tell of others who had stood there beneath its sheltering boughs.

When I read chapter 17 of Jeremiah, I am reminded of Camden's tree. Jeremiah spoke of a man whose heart had departed from the Lord, a person who would rather trust in another man than in God. He likened this man to a juniper tree growing in the desert or the "parched places in the wilderness" (Jeremiah 17:5–6). Then he spoke of a man that trusted in the Lord, and whose hope the Lord is. "He shall be as a tree planted by the waters, and that spreadeth out her roots by the river, and shall not see when heat cometh, but her leaf shall be green; and shall not be careful in the year of drought, neither shall cease from yielding fruit" (Jeremiah 17:8). I love the thought of the Lord whose hope is constantly flowing—offering refuge from heat, faith in time of drought, and fruit in every season. My thoughts turn to the blessings of protection, guidance, sustenance, and, then, to hope.

Can you think of someone whose hope the Lord is? How would you describe them?

"Blessed is that man that *trusteth* in the Lord, and whose *hope* the Lord is" (Jeremiah 17:7; emphasis added). There are days when the only thing that has gotten me through is my trust in the Lord and an unfailing hope in His ability to protect, guide, and provide sustenance for me and for my family. There are moments when the only thing that has kept me standing in the intense storms that surround me are the roots that stretch deep to find the Living Water. These are roots that stem from trust, that reach toward hope. Hope is an unspeakable gift. It is what sustains the soul in moments that would otherwise destroy us. Hope is what carries us through the places we could not get through on our own. Hope starts as a simple seed and then stretches its roots deep to flowing waters and its boughs high to heaven's reaching.

That's what happens when a tree is planted by the waters: Roots stretch deep and boughs reach high. Someday, perhaps, I will grow old and weathered, with roots spreading and branches reaching. Maybe a young boy will say of me, "I have to show you one of my favorite people; you will love her."

"What am I going to love about her?" the person might ask.

He will reply, "You're just going to love her." Then, when they come around the bend and see me standing there, perhaps they will recognize me as the person the boy was speaking of and think to themselves, "Oh, I *do* love her." They may not know why, exactly, but I hope they will see in me the kind of person whose hope the Lord is.

Hope in Thine End

Can contentment be found in captivity?

Can peace be found in the midst of great trial?

In the twenty-ninth chapter of Jeremiah we read of a group of people who were about to be carried away captive from Jerusalem into Babylon. How long would this period of captivity last? The Lord counseled the people, "Build ye houses, and dwell in them; and plant gardens, and eat the fruit of them; Take ye wives, and beget sons and daughters; and take wives for your sons, and give your daughters to husbands, that they may bear sons and daughters; *that ye may be increased there, and not diminished*" (Jeremiah 29:5–6; emphasis added).

Obviously these people are about to spend a lot of time in that place of refinement—enough time to build houses, plant gardens, marry, and raise children and grandchildren. This news must have been worrisome to the people, for immediately they knew this refinement process wasn't going to last just a couple of years. They would have to wait on the Lord, which meant they would have to trust His timing. The Lord gave them some important counsel: Through that period of trial He wanted them to experience an increase and not be diminished. Is the same lesson applicable in our own lives? Can we experience growth through trial? Can we experience an increase?

Next the Lord said, "Seek the peace of the city whither I have caused you to be carried away captives, and pray unto the Lord for it: for in the peace thereof shall ye have peace" (Jeremiah 29:7). The footnote for *peace* defines the Greek translation of the word as *contentment.* Knowing that this period of their lives would be challenging and that it would last a long time, the Lord encouraged them to pray to receive peace.

How hard would it have been to find contentment within the captivity? It is difficult to be content with the place where you are when it's not the place where you want to be. The last counsel the Lord gave Jeremiah's people included a blessing: "For thus saith the Lord, That after seventy years be accomplished at Babylon I will visit you, and perform my good word toward you, in causing you to return to this place. *For I know the thoughts that I think toward you,* saith the Lord, thoughts of peace . . . *to give you an expected end.* Then shall ye call upon me, and ye shall go and pray unto me, and I will hearken unto you. And ye shall seek me, and find me, when ye shall search for me with *all* your heart. And I will be found of you" (Jeremiah 29:10–14; emphasis added).

Seventy years is a long time. The people were in a place that was far from home, held captive by an unfamiliar people. But the Lord did not leave them without hope. He gave them a wonderful promise. Even though they would experience that trial for seventy years, the Lord promised they would not be forgotten. He would keep them in His thoughts. He promised to send peace, to answer their prayers, and to always be found by them. There was only one condition on their part—they had to seek for Him with all their heart. Not just a part of the heart. He wanted all of it.

Have you ever been in a trial that seemed like it would never end? Have you prayed to find peace within the trial? Did that experience teach you about what it means to trust in the Lord's timing? I'm thinking of a time when several unexpected events led to my husband's unemployment. It was a scary time. The first thing he did was ask for a priesthood blessing. The counsel from the blessing was clear, "The Lord has something in mind for you. Be patient. Wait." So we waited. And while we waited, Greg took care of the list of "honey-do's" I had been keeping for several years. When he finished the list and there was still no job on the horizon, we began to worry. Greg asked for another priesthood blessing. The counsel was the same, "The Lord has something in mind for you. Be patient. Wait."

Waiting is hard. By the end of January, things began to look desperate. We prayed fervently that the Lord would speed things up. Again we turned to the Lord. Again the counsel was the same, "The Lord has something in mind for you. Be patient. Wait."

> Have you ever been in a trial that seemed like it would never end? How does this verse bring you peace? "For I know the thoughts that I think toward you, . . . thoughts of peace . . . to give you an expected end."

Finally, at the end of March we stumbled upon a business opportunity. Things fell into place faster than we could have ever anticipated. We bought a business from a woman whose husband had just passed away from cancer. As my husband was talking to her about the events of her life over the last several months, she began to talk about the last few weeks of January, the weeks right before her husband passed away. As she spoke, my husband remembered how desperate those weeks had been for us, as we prayed fervently that the Lord would speed things up. During those same weeks, the woman's family had been praying too, that the Lord would slow things down so they would have more time together as a family, so the kids would have more time with their dad.

As my husband told me that story, it was a defining moment in my life. I learned what it meant to trust the Lord's timing. The Lord knew what was happening in both of our lives. He knew our family was going to be okay. He was orchestrating the events of that time period so things would be best for both families.

We just needed to trust Him, and in doing so, we would be led to find peace within the trial, contentment within the captivity, and grace within the wilderness place.

One of my favorite promises in Jeremiah is found in the footnote of a word in Jeremiah 29:11, "For I know the thoughts that I think toward you, . . . thoughts of peace . . . to give you an expected end." If you follow the footnote for *end,* it leads to Jeremiah 31:17, which reads, "And there is hope in thine end."

Great comfort comes from His promise that there will be hope in the end. No matter what the end brings, He will be there.

He is that hope.

still Abide

I have a favorite flower, which blooms only once a year. From the moment the first hint of green escapes from brown dirt until heavy buds hang on spindly stems, the anticipation begins filling my heart. If you were to ask me why I love these flowers so much, I think this would be my reply: They keep back nothing. The soft, sweet petals bursting from seemingly unyielding constraints never cease to delight me. Their fragrance can fill an entire room with a penetrating softness that somehow reaches right into my heart. Spring brings with it the promise of their coming. I have a special crystal cut-glass vase that was my grandmother's. It is reserved specifically for these, my favorite flowers. I only use it this one time a year. The flowers will travel room to room with me for as long as they are in bloom. When I am cooking, they are in the kitchen windowsill; when I am writing, they are there next to me on the desk; and every evening I carry them into my bedroom and set them carefully on my nightstand next to my bed. When I breathe deep, the soft, sweet fragrance fills me up all the way into the depths of my heart.

These flowers are hard to come by. They can't be purchased from the corner grocery store. I wonder, could it be the waiting that makes me love the flowers so much? Because every year it is the same: My heart waits for springtime and the promise that the peonies will bloom again.

Perhaps the same can be said about the sweet, tender-mercy

moments from the Lord that come after the waiting, springing forth from seemingly unyielding constraints, reaching down into the depths of our hearts.

Jeremiah speaks of a moment like this that came after the people had pled to know what the Lord would have them do in their confinement, before the blessings came. There, within the waiting, Jeremiah the prophet said to the people, "I have heard you; behold, I will pray unto the Lord your God according to your words; and it shall come to pass, that whatsoever thing the Lord shall answer you, I will declare it unto you; *I will keep nothing back from you*. . . . And [he] said unto them, Thus saith the Lord, the God of Israel . . . *If ye will still abide* in this land, then will I build you . . . and I will plant you. . . . Be not afraid . . . for I am with you to save you . . . and I will shew mercies unto you" (Jeremiah 42:4, 9–12; emphasis added). If ye will still abide, "I will perform that good thing which I have promised" (Jeremiah 33:14).

"If ye will still abide in this land, then will I build you. . . . Be not afraid . . . for I am with you to save you . . . and I will shew mercies unto you." When have you experienced this in your life?

I am reminded of the peonies whose sweet fragrance abides with me in every room. So it is with the Lord.

Abide with me! Fast falls the eventide;
The darkness deepens. Lord, with me abide!
When other helpers fail and comforts flee,
Help of the helpless, oh, abide with me!
("Abide with Me," *Hymns,* no. 166)

There will be moments of waiting. There will be times when all that we hope for seems bound by unyielding constraints. But ours is a Lord of tender mercies. He will perform that good thing which He has promised.

He will keep nothing back.

For this moment, still abide.

The Women That Stood By

"Then all the men which knew that their wives had burned incense unto other gods, *and all the women that stood by,* a great multitude . . . answered Jeremiah, saying, As for the word that thou hast spoken unto us in the name of the Lord, we will not hearken unto thee. But we will certainly do whatsoever thing goeth forth out of our own mouth" (Jeremiah 44:15–17; emphasis added).

I was caught off guard by the second sentence in that verse, *all the women that stood by.* It struck me deeply that the women who simply stood by and watched were as wrong as the women who had chosen to worship other gods. They stood by those who were not loyal to the prophet. In this case, the women who stood by and watched the worship of other gods had made a choice that would have negative consequences.

In the chapters that follow, Jeremiah recounts the devastation that followed the army of Babylon—the very destruction he had prophesied about. At that time, each of those "women who stood by" learned an important lesson: Jeremiah was, in fact, a prophet. All along he had been speaking for the Lord.

Instead of being "women that stood by" as others' wives burned incense unto other gods, why didn't they choose to stand by the prophet?

On the other hand, President Gordon B. Hinckley spoke of the good and faithful servants who have carried forward the work of the

Lord from the beginning. "They were present in the home of Peter Whitmer when the Church was organized. They were among *the few who stood by the Prophet* in the troubled days of the New York period of the Church. . . . *They stood by the Prophet* in Liberty Jail. . . . They drained the swamps of Commerce to create Nauvoo the Beautiful. . . . They were with Joseph at Carthage. They mourned his death and rallied to the leadership of the Twelve. With mobs at their backs they abandoned their homes and temple and faced the Iowa winter. . . . [In the Salt Lake Valley] they grubbed sagebrush; fought crickets; labored and prayed; built homes, churches, and temples to their God. Through all of this long odyssey there were those who were not loyal, some few who were traitors, who were betrayers, but they were a small minority. *Honor be to those who stood firm,* and to their wives who worked beside them" ("The Good and Faithful Servants," 49).

What is one way you could stand by the prophet today?

There is an important lesson here, a contrast between those who stood by the prophet and those who did not.

All the days of my life I want to be known as one of the few who stood by the prophet. *Honor be to those who stood firm.* May we honor them by choosing to still stand firm today.

The Holder of the Bow

I love the call to action found in chapter 51 of Jeremiah: "The Lord hath brought forth our righteousness: . . . Make bright the arrows; gather the shields: . . . Set up the standard . . . make the watch strong" (Jeremiah 51:10–12).

It is not hard to visualize the preparation taking place for the battle at hand: the gathering of the shields, the setting up of the standards along the walls, the strengthening of the watchtowers, and the sending up of the watchmen. But it is the line about making the arrows bright that catches my attention. It makes me think that just gathering the arrows was not enough; there was work to be done in making sure the arrows were ready for the battle. They had to be made bright. I want to know more about this brightness.

Perhaps it was the responsibility of the holder of the bow to make sure his arrows were prepared. In trying to research more about the process, I stumbled upon a quote from Elder Jeffrey R. Holland. Suddenly the lesson turned from physical arrows used in warfare to spiritual arrows and the battles that rage in the hearts of men today. "We anxiously watch that arrow in flight and know all the evils that can deflect its course after it has left our hand, nevertheless we take courage in remembering that the most important mortal factor in determining that arrow's destination will be the stability, strength, and unwavering certainty of the holder of the bow" ("A Prayer for the Children," 87).

> How bright is your arrow? Where does your stability come from? Where do you turn for strength? In what areas is your certainty unwavering?

Could each of us today be considered a holder of the bow? We live in a world where the evil that surrounds us can deflect the course of our arrows. Do we have the stability, strength, and unwavering certainty that Elder Holland speaks of? Perhaps we could ask ourselves three questions:

Where does my stability come from?

Where do I turn for strength?

In what areas is my certainty unwavering?

If the most important factor in determining the destination of our arrow rests upon those three things, then discovering the answers to those questions becomes crucial. As I consider my answers, I discover something important—what lies beneath the stability, the strength, and the certainty is the very essence of what I believe.

Every Morning

Most mornings I go for a walk. It gives me time to think.

On the mornings when things aren't going particularly well, I like to walk by myself so I can pray as I go. Sometimes my prayer echoes the thoughts of Jeremiah: "Thou hast removed my soul far off from peace. . . . My strength and my hope is perished . . . remembering mine affliction and my misery. . . . My soul hath them still in remembrance, and is humbled in me" (Lamentations 3:17–20). It never seems to fail: Once my soul gets in its humble place, my eyes come open and I begin to see things I might not have noticed before.

Every new morning it is the same. I notice His beauty surrounding me—I hear the brook flowing and the birds chirping. I feel the breeze on my face and the warmth of the sun on my shoulders. Then finally, somewhere within, my heart begins to swell with gratitude. There, within the gratitude, comes the whisper of a great truth: If He is the creator of all this goodness and the designer of all that surrounds me, if He gave attention to the detail of the smallest white blossom and added a brilliant yellow flower to the top of what most would consider a simple weed, if He shaped trees whose giant boughs would offer shade from intense heat and grasses that would whisper gently in the wind, *then what might He do with my life?*

Through His compassion and His mercy, might He take this soul that longs for peace and prosperity, that yearns for strength and hope, that cries within from affliction and sometimes even misery, and make it something more? Could He create goodness? Could He give attention to the small details and add brilliance to the parts that seem too simple? Might He offer refuge from the intensity? Could He whisper gentle words of inspiration and counsel along the way?

What mercies and compassions from the Lord can you recall to your mind?

As my soul becomes more humble, my eyes come open and I see the things I haven't noticed before.

His compassion. His mercies. His hand creating and defining my life, adding brilliance, refuge, inspiration, and beauty. I am becoming new. "This I recall to my mind, therefore have I hope. It is of the Lord's mercies that we are not consumed, because his compassions fail not. They are new every morning" (Lamentations 3:21–23).

A Prophet Among Them

Several months ago I went for a walk with my husband in Cancun, Mexico. We walked around a bend and came upon the most interesting wall I have ever seen. It was not a beautiful wall. The structure was made out of tan cinder blocks held together with gray mortar. The mortar job was one of the messiest I have ever seen.

The gray cement was not confined to its place, but dripped all the way down the side of the wall. Across the top of the wall someone had placed shards of broken glass and mirrors to dissuade anyone from climbing over.

Reading Ezekiel reminded me of the wall. "And one built up a wall, and, lo, others daubed it with untempered morter: Say unto them which daub it with untempered morter, that it shall fall. . . . Lo, when the wall is fallen, shall it not be said unto you, Where is the daubing wherewith ye have daubed it?" (Ezekiel 13:10–12).

It makes you wonder, what was the "untempered morter," the "daubing"? A hint can be found in Ezekiel 22:28, "And her prophets have daubed them with untempered morter, seeing vanity, and divining lies unto them, saying, Thus saith the Lord God, when the Lord hath not spoken."

The "untempered morter" came from false prophets who spoke lies, who were filled with self-absorption and pride, who said they were speaking for God. They were not. A wall built with this type of mortar cannot stand. It lacks strength, it is messy, and it is built to dissuade. I don't want to make the same mistake, so I ask myself, What is my mortar?

I can't help but think of the words of holy prophets—those who speak to us today and those who have gone before. Their words become our mortar. As we study them, we discover the evidences of the hand of the Lord in the lives of His people. We learn how the Lord speaks to His people, and we come to learn of His ways. These evidences become the strength behind our mortar.

What is one lesson you have learned from the prophet that has added strength to your mortar?

Consider these verses from Ezekiel: "I do send thee unto them; and thou shalt say unto them, Thus saith the Lord God. And they, whether they will hear, or whether they will forbear, (for they are a rebellious house,) *yet shall know that there hath been a prophet among them*" (Ezekiel 2:4–5; emphasis added). They would know that there was a prophet of God right in their midst, a prophet whose sole responsibility was to teach the words of the Lord—a prophet who had the ability to strengthen their mortar. Yet some would choose not to hear him.

I know that there is a prophet among us. I want to listen and hear his words so that the mortar I build my testimony with will hold firm.

stand in the gap

One summer our family had the opportunity to spend a weekend high up in the mountains of Coalville, Utah. On one of the days we volunteered to help clear a hiking trail. Have you ever been to a remote area where the overgrowth of the vegetation is so thick that it prevents you from being able to walk through? That is what had happened to this hiking trail. Trees had fallen into the trail, tall weeds had grown up in the path, giant bushes were crowding in from the sides—the thick vegetation had overtaken the hiking trail, creating a hedge.

In the book of Ezekiel the Lord speaks of the great battle of the last days. He worried that the Saints would not prepare themselves sufficiently to be protected. "Ye have not gone up into the gaps, neither made up the hedge for the house of Israel to stand in the battle in the day of the Lord" (Ezekiel 13:5). As with the trail in Coalville, a hedge would make the area impassable. In a way, the thick hedge would act as a protection, a barrier—nothing would be able to pass through. However, where there were gaps in the hedge, there would be a lack of protection, a place for the enemy to enter in. In order to compensate for the gaps, Ezekiel "sought for a man among them, that should make up the hedge, and stand in the gap before . . . the land . . . *but I found none*" (Ezekiel 22:30; emphasis added).

This scripture haunts me. Why could he not find a man to stand in the gap? Why was there no one to offer strength against the enemy in the places where the hedge didn't provide enough protection?

We live in the era Ezekiel prophesied of. The battle rages fiercely around us, and if we look carefully we might be able to detect the gaps in the hedge. Someone needs to fill the gaps. Someone needs to make up the hedge.

What would we have to do to qualify ourselves for that position? What would help us to be found of the Lord in the moment when He needs us most?

The book of Ezekiel lists the things that *won't* qualify us to stand in the gap:

- follow foolish prophets
- take counsel from those who speak lies, and see vanity
- use oppression, persecution, cruelty
- exercise robbery or deception
- vex the poor and needy
- oppress the stranger wrongfully

Perhaps if we look at the opposite of these characteristics, we might find clues as to what we *should* do:

- follow the prophet
- take counsel from those who speak the truth
- let our first response be kindness
- live with integrity
- serve, reach out, assist

It is an interesting set of requirements. I find myself questioning, Are these the qualities that are characteristic of a warrior? At first glance they do not seem like the requirements I would expect for someone who would be prepared to stand in a battle, to make up for the hedge, or even to go up into the gaps. Further consideration helps me to realize that we might not fully understand the nature of the battle that rages around us. If our strength is to be found through obtaining counsel and learning kindness, integrity, and charity, then we won't have to look far for instruction. Our best resource for the most recent counsel pertaining to the war that rages around us is easy to obtain. Within the pages of the general conference issues of the *Ensign* we can learn about kindness, integrity, charity, and other qualities that will help us to become the type of person qualified to make up the hedge and to stand in the gaps. This chapter in Ezekiel is a good reminder.

What is one piece of counsel from the most recent general conference that would prepare you to stand in the gap?

In our family, we have a general conference tradition. Each of us chooses one piece of counsel to work on for the six months following conference. We have a conference wall where we hang the quotes so we can see them every single day. Every time we see them, it becomes a reminder that we need to work on making that counsel part of who we are becoming, to fill the gaps, and to make up for what we are lacking.

So that we can be found of the Lord.

showers of Blessing

"Thus saith the Lord God . . . should not the shepherds feed the flocks? . . . The diseased have ye not strengthened, neither have ye healed that which was sick, neither have ye bound up that which was broken, neither have ye brought again that which was driven away, neither have ye sought that which was lost. . . . And they were scattered, because there is no shepherd" (Ezekiel 34:2, 4–5). I picture the sheep described here and my heart hurts for the sick one that was not healed, the broken one that was not bound up, the one that was not strengthened, the lost one, and the one that was driven away. Why was there no one to care for them?

My sister raises sheep. One day, one of her ewes delivered three baby lambs. Finding it too hard to care for all three babies, the mother began to neglect the smallest lamb. My sister was aware that this might happen. She had been watching over her flock. So, even though it would require sacrifice, she decided to mother this little lamb. She made a makeshift bed for it in her kitchen and let it follow her all through her house. The little lamb's favorite place to be was right under my sister's feet; she felt safe there, watched over, and cared for.

My sister named her Joy. It made me happy that the one who was broken, driven away, and uncared for was given such a happy name.

The experience of watching my sister care for her little lamb made my heart tender toward the way this chapter in Ezekiel ends. After expressing His unhappiness with the shepherds of Israel, the Lord extended a beautiful promise: "For thus saith the Lord God; Behold, I, even I, will both search my sheep, and seek them out. As a shepherd seeketh out his flock . . . so will I seek out my sheep, and will deliver them out of all places where they have been scattered in the cloudy and dark day . . . and feed them upon the mountains of Israel by the rivers. . . . I will feed them in a good pasture. . . . *I will seek that which was lost, and bring again that which was driven away, and will bind up that which was broken, and will strengthen that which was sick* . . . and I will make them and the places round about my hill a blessing; and I will cause the shower to come down in his season; there shall be showers of blessing. . . . Thus shall they know that I the Lord their God am with them" (Ezekiel 34:11–14, 16, 26, 30; emphasis added).

"I will seek that which was lost, and bring again that which was driven away, and will bind up that which was broken, and will strengthen that which was sick." When have you experienced this?

There is One who is watching over us on our cloudy and dark days. He will seek us when we are lost, bring us back when we are driven away, bind us up when we are broken, and give us strength beyond our own. Why does He do this? In Hebrews 12 we find the answer: "Who *for the joy that was set before him* endured the cross" (Hebrews 12:2; emphasis added).

Were we the joy that was set before Him?

His joy?

Maybe we could remember that in the moments when we feel uncared for, driven away, lost, or broken. We are His joy, upon whom He will send showers of blessing. We must sit at His feet. We will be safe there, watched over, and cared for.

For They Shall Be Healed

The vision in which a heavenly ministrant shows Ezekiel the temple started with this counsel: "Set thine heart upon all that I shall shew thee" (Ezekiel 40:4). Perhaps as we prepare to learn from this vision we could do the same.

The temple "had a wall round about . . . to make a separation between the sanctuary and the profane place" (Ezekiel 42:20). "Teach my people the difference between the holy and profane" (Ezekiel 44:23).

The footnotes for these verses substitute *common* for *profane* and *sacred* for *holy*. So, to begin with, we are taught that there is a difference between the common and profane as contrasted with the holy and sacred, and that we must learn to make a separation between those two ideals to find the sanctuary within. It is an important concept because our greatest blessings can be found on the inside of the wall round about, in the place that is holy or sacred. It is "the place of my throne, and the place of the soles of my feet, where I will dwell in the midst of the children of Israel for ever" (Ezekiel 43:7). In that sanctuary, that place of refuge or safety, we enter the place of Christ—who is the source of all healing. It is a promise we can set our hearts upon.

Next we are taught the importance of immersing ourselves fully in that holy place. In the vision, Ezekiel walked through the waters that issued out from under the threshold of the house, "and he brought me through the waters; the waters were to the ankles . . . and brought me through the waters; the waters were to the knees . . . and brought me through; the waters were to the loins . . . and it was a river that I could not pass over: for the waters were risen, waters to swim in, *a river that could not be passed over*" (Ezekiel 47:3–5; emphasis added). My thoughts fill with memories of moments I have spent in the temple—especially the times when just stepping in up to my ankles was not sufficient. The times I remember most are the moments when I have fully immersed myself into that sanctuary which is holy, sacred. In these moments, the temple has been a place of refuge and safety for my heart. As I have turned my heart to Christ in that sanctuary, the healing has come. Blessings can be found within those walls, pouring out, spilling over, and overflowing.

Toward the end of Ezekiel's vision of the temple, just after the lesson of fully being immersed in the water, an interesting thing happens: The living waters that fill the temple and spill out of the east side of the holy place flow down to the Dead Sea. A friend who has been to the Dead Sea taught me a remarkable lesson about how it relates to this chapter of Ezekiel. The area surrounding the Dead Sea is lifeless desert. It is dry. It is hot. It is miserable. The Dead Sea supports no life. The salt content is so high it allows nothing to grow or thrive. The waters burn the smallest paper cut on your skin; they are disgusting to the taste; and they become almost unbearable if even a drop gets in your eye. The sea may look refreshing against the sand dunes, but it is deceiving. In addition to all of this, it also happens to be the lowest spot of land on the whole earth, and it is lowering with each passing year. It is not only dead, it is continually dying. You cannot find a more lifeless and helpless spot on earth.

But Ezekiel speaks of a remarkable promise: "These waters issue out toward the east country, and go down into the desert, and go into the sea: which being brought forth into the sea, *the waters shall be healed.*

. . . And *every thing shall live whither the river cometh*" (Ezekiel 47:8–9; emphasis added).

The waters that flow from the temple will heal the Dead Sea, and "every thing shall live." That is perhaps one of the most unbelievable lessons in the Old Testament because the common eye would see water that is not healable. But those who remember to separate the common from the sacred, to see the holy, will understand that the waters from the temple are symbolic of the healing power of Jesus Christ. They flow from the temple—the sanctuary, the place of healing. It is a place where we can be completely immersed in healing, mercy, and grace, where the healing waters seem to find the spots that need them most.

How might you more fully set your heart on attending the temple?

The Atonement of Christ can heal anyone, anything, anytime. If these waters can heal the lowest, driest place on earth, then there is not a soul on earth who is out of reach of the flowing, healing power of Jesus. You can set your heart on that promise.

He can reach you in your lowest moments. He can give you refreshment in your driest hours. He can make you beautiful again. What once was dead can now sparkle with life.

I do believe those waters will one day flow from the source and touch every part of God's earth. But I also believe we can immerse ourselves in them now, in places of covenants. In places of mercy. In places of peace. In places of God. In His holy sanctuary.

weighed in the Balance

Earlier this year I had the opportunity to spend some time backstage in a theater that was unlike any I have visited before. What made it unique was the writing on the wall. Made of reddish tan bricks, the walls rose from floor to ceiling and spanned from left to right as far as the eye could see. Written on each individual brick was the name of a person who had performed on that stage, and the year that the person performed there.

The bricks were numbered and signed, and each contained a message that the person would be remembered for. I found myself captivated by them. I couldn't help but wonder what message I would have left as writing on the wall.

In the book of Daniel, Belshazzar the king had a great feast. He did not have a humble heart. He had lifted himself up against the Lord. On this particular evening he had poured wine for his guests into the vessels that had been stolen out of the house of the Lord. In the midst of this great feast a hand sent from God left writing on the wall, "MENE, MENE, TEKEL, UPHARSIN" (Daniel 5:25). A simple translation would read, "Numbered. Numbered. Weighed. Divided."

The king felt that there was more behind the message than just those three words. He sent for his wise men, but none could translate. So the queen suggested he call for Daniel. I love how she describes him: "There is a man in thy kingdom, in whom is the spirit of the holy gods; and in the days of thy father light and understanding and wisdom, like the wisdom of the gods, was found in him. . . . An excellent spirit, and knowledge, and understanding, interpreting of dreams, and shewing of hard sentences, and dissolving of doubts, were found in the same Daniel" (Daniel 5:11–12). So Daniel was brought before the king.

The first thing the king asked him was, "Art thou that Daniel . . . ? *I have even heard of thee,* that the spirit of the gods is in thee, and that light and understanding and excellent wisdom is found in thee. . . . *I have heard of thee,* that thou canst make interpretations, and dissolve doubts" (Daniel 5:13–14, 16; emphasis added). Daniel agreed to make known the interpretation of the dream to the king. He spoke of the king's father, Nebuchadnezzar, and his weaknesses and strengths. Then he spoke of King Belshazzar and the places where he was lacking in righteousness. He spoke with the Spirit of God. He spoke wisdom and brought light and understanding. He spoke hard sentences. He spoke knowledge. And then, dissolving doubt, he interpreted the writing on the wall.

Each of the three words written on the wall had a different interpretation, but it is the middle word that catches my full attention. "TEKEL; Thou art *weighed* in the balances, and art found wanting" (Daniel 5:27; emphasis added). There is an important lesson contained within this chapter. If you look carefully, you will see that two men were weighed in the balance. One was known for his drinking, his praise for the gods of gold, his prideful heart—he was known as a man who did not glorify God. The other was known for his excellent spirit, his light and understanding, his wisdom, his knowledge, his ability to dissolve doubt. Both were weighed in the balances, but only one was found wanting.

I love the six words King Belshazzar said of Daniel, *"I have even heard of thee."* I can't help but wonder: If people were to say, "Oh, I have heard of you . . ." how would they describe me? When I was weighed in the balances, would words such as those used to describe Daniel come to mind? What would I have to change in my life so that those words would describe me?

Sometimes, at the end of the day, I find myself going over all of the decisions and errands and tasks that have filled up each hour. Looking back at the whole of the day I often find myself wondering, when it is weighed in the balances, if there are parts of it that are found wanting. On those days I try to learn from my mistakes. To ask for an increase of the Spirit. To seek for more light, understanding, and knowledge. To ask myself the hard sentences.

Can you remember a time when the Savior brought balance to your life?

Sometimes I find myself wanting in my abilities as a mother, a wife, a friend. There are days I do not want to be remembered for. In those moments there is always one thing that dissolves my doubt. It is a scripture found in Isaiah 40:12. Speaking of the Savior, it asks, "Who hath measured the waters in the hollow of his hand, and meted out heaven with the span, and comprehended the dust of the earth in a measure, and weighed the mountains in scales, and the hills in a balance?"

I love to picture the Savior with the water of the earth cupped in one hand while the other hand spans the expanse of heaven. He knows instantly how to measure out the dust and to balance the mountains and hills.

If the Savior can handle all of that, I know that He can help me. He can bring my life into balance. If I turn to Him, He can add to my life understanding, light, knowledge, and wisdom. Then, hopefully, when people say, "Oh, I have heard of you . . ." in the moment when I am weighed in the balance, I will not be found wanting.

"Gather yourselves together, yea, gather together. . . .
The Lord thy God in the midst of thee is mighty;
he will save, he will rejoice over thee with joy."

ZEPHANIAH 2:1; 3:17

Invitations from

Jonah, Micah, Nahum, Habakkuk, Zephaniah, Haggai, and Malachi

O Sleeper, Arise

We all know the story of Jonah—the running away from Nineveh, the boat, the storm, the big fish, the three days in the belly. Remember that Jonah? I can't help but think about how Jonah's story in the Bible compares to Alma's story in the Book of Mormon.

Two prophets were called of God to cry repentance to very wicked cities: one to Nineveh, the other to Ammonihah. Persecution, failure, and possibly even death awaited them within the city walls. But the Lord had a purpose in mind for these two cities. He knew these men were capable of preaching the gospel with the Spirit. He knew the Spirit was capable of changing hearts. The difference in the two accounts is the way each prophet responded to the commandment of the Lord.

Jonah "rose up to flee" (Jonah 1:3). "After Alma had received his message from the angel of the Lord he *returned speedily* . . . [and] entered the city by another way" (Alma 8:18; emphasis added). In Alma's case, the Lord had prepared the way before him so that he could accomplish the great work in store. An angel had been sent. A man's heart was softened. A companion was waiting to assist in the work. In Jonah's case, the Lord had also prepared a way for him to accomplish the great work in store. The Lord sent the wind, caused a mighty tempest, and "*prepared* a great fish to swallow up Jonah" (Jonah 1:17; emphasis added).

Nothing can stop the work of the Lord. He will always prepare the way for His great work to be accomplished. If we act upon the direction we are given and allow the Spirit to be our guide, great blessings await us. We might feel overwhelmed by the task at hand. Frightened. Discouraged. We must remember that God will give us every chance to succeed. He will prepare the way for us to accomplish His great work, even if it requires unlikely adventures.

> Are there areas in which you are sleeping as the tempest rages around you? Are you missing out on a great work you could be performing on the Lord's behalf?

Just after Jonah fled to the ship, as the ship was being tossed by the great tempest in the sea, when Jonah was fast asleep "the shipmaster came to him, and said unto him . . . O sleeper? arise, call upon thy God" (Jonah 1:6). This verse caused me to analyze my own life. Are there areas in which I am sleeping as the tempest rages around me? Am I missing out on a great work I could be performing on the Lord's behalf within my family, my calling, or my circle of influence? If so, I need to arise—to move from the place where I am to a place that I need to be. Speedily.

I must call upon my God.

He knows the great work He has in store for me.

satisfied

It was as I sat in the dentist chair that I felt the regret.

The hard lemon candy that had seemed so appealing one morning several weeks ago really hadn't been worth it.

It hadn't been worth the dull toothache keeping me up at night. It hadn't been worth the cost of now repairing the damage. It hadn't been worth the time I was giving up to fix a big problem caused by a small, yellow piece of candy. The satisfaction from the sweet sugar had been momentary. The consequences of biting that hard piece of candy were lasting. Now I sat in the dentist's chair waiting for him to fix a problem I couldn't resolve on my own. In that moment, sitting in the chair, my lip growing numb, one thought kept running through my mind: As sweet as it was, that lemon drop just hadn't been worth it.

After I left the office, I read this verse in Micah. "Thou shalt eat, but not be satisfied; and thy casting down shall be in the midst of thee" (Micah 6:14). The footnote makes it easier to understand. "Thou shalt eat, but not be satisfied; and thy hunger shall be in thy inward parts." After my lemon-drop experience, I can sort of understand what it means to eat something and not be satisfied. But I don't think Micah was talking about lemon drops.

I think he was talking about spiritual hunger, the kind of hunger that is down deep inside your soul—the emptiness, the longing, the yearning for something more. Sometimes we try to take care of that hunger, that longing, that aching, with that which cannot satisfy. If we are not careful, our choice might cause us pain. It might come with a cost we are not willing to pay. It might even lead to greater hunger—emptiness that reaches deep into our inward parts.

> What gift from the Savior has satisfied the spiritual hunger of your inward parts?

The Savior knows how to satisfy our hungering, our yearning, and our aching. I have felt His ability to soothe the longing in my own life. I have seen Him heal the aching in the hearts of those I love. He understands our innermost longing. He knows our wants. He knows our needs. Only He can bring that which will satisfy. Through Him, we will become full.

A Strong Hold

A few weeks ago my daughter's friend went rappeling with a big group. Some of the group stood on the top of the mountain waiting for their turn; those who had already gone watched from below. One was assigned to hold the rope at the bottom. This post was crucial. His job was to hold the end of the rope as the climber descended down the face of the cliff. His dedication to the job ensured safety for the one who was attempting the descent. In essence, the person descending was placing his very survival in the hands of the one holding the rope.

On this particular day there were two different groups rappeling. As my daughter's friend descended, he heard a boy from the other group yell from the top of the cliff that he was about to start his descent. What the boy didn't know, because he couldn't see the bottom, was that the person assigned to hold the other end of his rope had left his post.

The boy jumped off the top of the cliff and fell 110 feet to the bottom with no one there to hold the other end of his rope. Miraculously, his life was spared. He sustained major injuries, but he lived. Sadly, the danger, the cries of fear, the excruciating pain could all have been prevented if someone had just kept a strong hold on the other end of the rope.

I love the message found in the book of Nahum, "The Lord is good, *a strong hold in the day of trouble;* and he knoweth them that trust in him" (Nahum 1:7; emphasis added). In moments of danger, fear, or pain, when it seems as if all of life is going downhill fast, we must never forget that the Lord stands waiting and watching, with a strong hold on the other end of the rope. He will not leave His post. In the day of trouble we must put our trust in Him. He will hold on to us until we arrive safely at the end. He knows us. If we rely on Him, He will not let us fall.

> "The Lord is good,
> a strong hold in the
> day of trouble."
> Can you remember
> a time when this was
> the case for you?

In His Holy Temple

One of the greatest lessons I have learned from the Old Testament is found in the imagery of the idols. Since idol worship is a recurring theme throughout all 1,184 pages of the Old Testament, I know that it must be a recurring theme now—a tradition handed down through generations. I do not want to follow their ways. "What profiteth the graven image that the maker thereof hath graven it. . . . Woe unto him that saith to the wood, Awake; to the dumb stone, Arise, it shall teach! Behold it is laid over with gold and silver, and there is no breath at all in the midst of it. *But the Lord is in his holy temple*" (Habakkuk 2:18–20; emphasis added). It seems ridiculous to us, I know. We cannot understand the devotion to these idols made of stone and wood and covered with gold and silver. We shake our heads and wonder how the people could be so ignorant. Their God was not in the wood or the stone, the silver or the gold, the works their hands had made—He was in the temple. Why did they waste their time worshipping a god that had no breath at all in the midst of it?

It is in the moments when I pray, asking that my eyes will be open to understand, that I discover my own ignorance. There is a temple less than ten minutes away from my home. The Lord is in that holy temple. And yet, my days are filled with maintaining that which I have paid for in gold and silver, and built up of wood and stone, and there is no breath at all in the midst of those things.

Someone once told me that the place where I devote most of my time is the place I worship most.

It is a hard question to ask the soul. Where is it that I devote most of my time? Don't get me wrong, I am not suggesting that we can't have beautiful homes, that we do not need vehicles to get us where we need to go, that an honest day of work is not admirable. But today I am reminding myself that the God I worship is in His holy temple, just minutes away from my home. I know where He is. His name is there on His house.

> There is a difference between temple work and temple worship. What is one blessing that comes from truly worshiping the Lord in His holy temple?

I need to balance my life in such a way that I am devoted to visiting Him—just as devoted as I am to the other important things in my life. There are places to go and people to see, jobs to attend to and children to raise, service to be given and scriptures to be read, and those are all good things. But the Lord *is* in His holy temple.

Perhaps sometime soon we could each find a moment to visit Him there.

gathering

Every time I see a bird's nest, my thoughts become captivated with the principle of gathering. It is a painstaking process, the mother bird's gathering of each piece of straw. She gathers it one piece at a time and then fits it carefully into the refuge she is building. Before the eggs can be settled within, before the babies burst out of their shells, before the constant peeping that signals new life and new hope, she gathers.

Seeking the perfect branch.

Seeking each piece of straw.

Creating a place of refuge.

The nest becomes a place that she will visit throughout the day and often sit in the midst of. Babies will come, and she will rejoice over them, and the morning will be filled with their songs of joy. But first, every year, it is the same—the process begins with the gathering. "Gather yourselves together, yea, gather together . . . before the day pass as the chaff, before the fierce anger of the Lord come upon you. . . . Seek ye the Lord . . . seek righteousness, seek meekness. . . . For the Lord . . . shall visit . . . even the Lord, is in the midst of thee. . . . The Lord thy God in the midst of thee is mighty; he will save, he will rejoice over thee with joy; he will rest in his love, he will joy over thee with singing. I will gather them. . . . At that time will I bring you again, even in the time that I gather you" (Zephaniah 2:1–3, 7; 3:15, 17–18, 20).

Within the building of the nest and the words of Zephaniah I learn a lesson. It is based on the doctrine of gathering. The mother bird's gathering of straw for the nest is much like the gathering of the Lord as He guides us, one by one, to find the place of refuge, a place where He will visit and be found in the midst thereof, a place where we can rejoice and rest in His love.

What blessings have come to you as you have gathered together with the saints of God?

"It is not surprising then that God urges us to gather so that He can bless us. He wants us to gather into families. He has established classes, wards, and branches and commanded us to meet together often. In those gatherings, which God has designed for us, lies our great opportunity. . . . We will move together in power to go wherever God would have us go and to become what He wants us to be" (Henry B. Eyring, "Our Hearts Knit as One," 69, 71).

consider your ways

The people of Haggai's day had become sidetracked on their journey to discipleship. They were meant to be building the temple, but they lost focus somewhere along the way. The Lord said to the people: "*Consider your ways.* Ye have sown much, and bring in little; ye eat, but ye have not enough; ye drink, but ye are not filled with drink; ye clothe you, but there is none warm; and he that earneth wages earneth wages to put it into a bag with holes. Thus saith the Lord of hosts; *Consider your ways*" (Haggai 1:5–7; emphasis added).

This description sounds a lot like our day. Our world is filled with people who work hard but bring in little, who are unsatisfied and lack a feeling of fulfillment. Unfortunately, the illustration of money slipping away is an idea that many of us can relate to. Perhaps we too should consider our ways.

The Lord explains the problem, "Ye looked for much, and, lo, it came to little; . . . the heaven over you is stayed from dew, and the earth is stayed from her fruit" (Haggai 1:9–10). Somehow these people had lost focus. What accounted in their eyes as much was in reality little. They had laid aside the most important thing. Building the temple would have allowed the Lord to remain forefront in their lives. Without Him, the dew from heaven and the fruit of the earth were stayed.

Dew is often used figuratively to represent inspiration from heaven.

When the Lord and His house became of lesser importance to the people of Haggai, inspiration from heaven also decreased, and the people were left to their own means. Their lives lacked the blessing that comes through inspiration. The Bible Dictionary explains that the worldly behavior of the people had brought about a curse on their labor and their increase (see Bible Dictionary, s.v. "Haggai"). As unfortunate as that is, it makes sense, and we are led to wonder if the same is true in our day.

But the Lord did not forget His people. He stirred up their spirits in remembrance, and He was forgiving. As soon as they laid the foundation for the temple, the Lord became their focus, and their lives began to change for the better. "Consider now from this day and upward . . . even from the day that the foundation of the Lord's temple was laid, consider it. Is the seed yet in the barn? yea, as yet the vine, and the fig tree, and the pomegranate, and the olive tree . . . from this day will I bless you" (Haggai 2:18–19).

consider your ways.
Do your ways lead you to seek inspiration on a daily basis? What can you do to make the Lord a first priority in your life?

Their willingness to turn to the Lord, to make Him a first priority, allowed Him to send great blessings they otherwise might not have obtained. Because their thoughts were focused on Him, they were able to receive inspiration for their lives. Is it possible that this counsel would work in our lives? What if we were to ask ourselves that same question? *Consider your ways.*

From this day He will bless you.

A Blessing Poured Out

There are several verses in Malachi that we are very familiar with. But hidden within those verses there are two words that I had never noticed until just recently—two words that completely changed my heart on the subject of paying tithes. If you look in the footnotes for Malachi 3:8–10, you will discover the two words I am talking about—*gratitude* and *generosity*. The first is found in the footnote for verse 8, "Will a man rob God?" The word contained in this footnote is *ingratitude.* It leads me to wonder what place gratitude has in the payment of our tithes. What exactly does gratitude have to do with tithing?

It has been about ten months since my husband saw a boy whom we had mentored for half a decade standing on the sidewalk with all of his belongings. His family was being evicted from their house. The boy had nowhere to live. "What should I do with Garett?" Greg called to ask me after he had pulled over to the side of the road.

"Bring him home," I said. I'll be honest, I didn't know how long he would make it at our house. The boundaries, the structure, the unfamiliar surroundings day in and day out seemed like too much for him to conform to.

We took it a day at a time. He started going to church. He was home and in bed by eleven. Slowly, he began turning his life around. He got a job . . . and he started paying tithing. One day he asked me, "Why do I pay tithing, again? I don't get it. Aren't I supposed to be seeing blessings?" He was serious, thoughtful, trying to understand.

"Do you see the blessings?" I asked him.

"I don't think so," he replied.

"Do you have a job?" I asked.

"Yes."

"Have you *ever* had a job before?"

"No."

"Do you have a roof over your head? A comfortable place to sleep? Clothes to wear? Do you feel safe here? Welcome? Do you feel happy?"

As he began nodding his head, I asked again, "Do you *see* the blessings?"

He tilted his head, reflecting, and then I watched the understanding come into his eyes. "I *am* blessed," he said. "I *am* happy. Is that what it feels like when you pay your tithing?" In that moment it became clear to me that gratitude pays a huge part in the payment of our tithes.

The Lord asks us to prove Him. He promises to open the windows of heaven, to pour out a blessing that there will not be room enough to receive. But what if He is pouring out blessings and we don't recognize them there?

Every so often, when I remember, after I have filled out the tithing slip and placed it in the little gray envelope, I pause. If I am in a place where it is appropriate, I offer up a silent prayer of gratitude for the opportunity I have to pay tithing and for the blessings that surround us everywhere—even the ones I may forget to acknowledge.

The second word you will notice in the footnotes is *generosity.* It is linked to the phrase, "open . . . the windows of heaven." Those verses in Malachi remind us how generous the Lord is with us. A story of President Henry D. Moyle, told by President James E. Faust, taught me the importance of being generous with the Lord:

"As I grew up out in the Cottonwood area of the Salt Lake Valley, President Henry D. Moyle was our stake president. Years passed and I became bishop of our ward. President Moyle, in the intervening years, was called to the Council of the Twelve and later to the First Presidency. Like the other faithful members of the ward, President Moyle always came to tithing settlement. Invariably each year he would make out a check for the balance of his tithing. As he handed me the check he always said, 'Bishop, this is a full tithe and a little bit more because that's the way we have been blessed'" ("Doing the Best Things," 41–42). His story is a lesson on generosity.

How might feeling gratitude and generosity as you pay your tithing leave an impression on your heart?

Sometimes paying tithing becomes routine—I write out the check, put it in the envelope, and hand it to a member of the bishopric. In the process I forget two important steps: the gratitude and the generosity.

I want the payment of my tithes to leave an impression on my heart so that I won't ever forget that I *am* blessed, that I *am* happy. I want to approach the Lord with gratitude and with generosity.

Because that's the way I have been blessed.

conclusion

This has been a very sweet and much-needed journey. I began the experience reaching and yearning for growth. I opened my heart wide to allow Him more room for the molding, shaping, and leading that needed to take place there. Looking back, I realize how far I have come. Now, as I thumb through the pages of the Old Testament, I see names that have become familiar and stories that have left an impression on my heart. Within each of the chapters I recognize a familiar theme.

Sometimes you just need to know the Lord is near.

Sometimes the journey seems long, and although the scenery is breathtaking and the companions pleasant, there are moments when you might wonder if you can take another step. Perhaps it is the heavy load you shoulder. Maybe it is the fear of what lies around the next corner. It could be that you're not quite ready for the detour, or the change of course, or the incline that lies ahead.

Do you know those moments?

The Old Testament taught me that there is One who is with us through every journey, through every wilderness place, and through every mountain moment. He is there through the detours, and the changes of course, and the occasions that cause us to climb vertically. He is the Deliverer, Jehovah. He is Jesus Christ.

He will be with us on our very worst days.

He will help us get through the longest nights.

He will bring peace through the times of heartache.

And in the moments when we long for deliverance, He will not leave our side.

But now thus saith the Lord that created thee . . .
Fear not: for I have redeemed thee,
I have called thee by thy name;
thou art mine.
When thou passest through the waters, I will be with thee;
and through the rivers, they shall not overflow thee:
when thou walkest through the fire, thou shalt not be burned;
neither shall the flame kindle upon thee.
For I am the Lord thy God,
the Holy One of Israel,
thy Saviour: . . .
Since thou wast precious in my sight . . . I have loved thee. . . .
Fear not: for I am with thee.
(Isaiah 43:1–5)

He lives, He loves us, and He will deliver us.

Of this, I am certain.

sources

Benson, Ezra Taft. "In His Steps." *Ensign,* September 1988, 2–6.

Busche, F. Enzio. "Unleashing the Dormant Spirit." Brigham Young University Devotional address delivered May 14, 1996. Accessed at http://speeches.byu.edu.

Corbett, Don Cecil. *Mary Fielding Smith, Daughter of Britain.* Salt Lake City: Deseret Book, 1974.

Dew, Sheri. "Are We Not All Mothers?" *Ensign,* November 2001, 96–98.

Edersheim, Alfred. *The Bible History: Old Testament.* 7 vols. Grand Rapids, Michigan: Wm. B. Eerdmans Publishing Company, 1956.

Eyring, Henry B. "Our Hearts Knit as One." *Ensign,* November 2008, 68–71.

Faust, James E. "Doing the Best Things in the Worst Times." *Ensign,* August 1984, 41–43.

Hinckley, Gordon B. "The Good and Faithful Servants." *Ensign,* November 1984, 48–49.

Holland, Jeffrey R. "A Handful of Meal and a Little Oil." *Ensign,* May 1996, 29–31.

———. "'An High Priest of Good Things to Come.'" *Ensign,* November 1999, 36–38.

———. "The Ministry of Angels." *Ensign,* November 2008, 29–31.

———. "A Prayer for the Children." *Ensign,* May 2003, 85–87.

Hymns of The Church of Jesus Christ of Latter-day Saints. Salt Lake City: The Church of Jesus Christ of Latter-day Saints, 1985.

Madsen, Truman G. *The Highest in Us.* Salt Lake City: Deseret Book, 1978.

Monson, Thomas S. "May You Have Courage." *Ensign,* May 2009, 123–27.

———. "To the Rescue." *Ensign,* May 2001, 48–50.

Tanner, Susan W. "My Soul Delighteth in the Things of the Lord." *Ensign,* May 2008, 81–83.

Taylor, Bonnie, ed. *J. Golden Kimball: December 1891–April 1938.* N.p.: Latter-Day Publishing, 2007.

Uchtdorf, Dieter F. "Lift Where You Stand." *Ensign,* November 2008, 53–56.

———. "We Are Doing a Great Work and Cannot Come Down." *Ensign,* May 2009, 59–62.

———. "Your Happily Ever After." *Ensign,* May 2010, 124–27.

Wirthlin, Joseph B. "Come What May, and Love It." *Ensign,* November 2008, 26–28.

Index